Let Us Python Solutions

7th Edition

Yashavant Kanetkar
Aditya Kanetkar

www.bpbonline.com

Seventh Revised & Updated Edition 2025

FIRST EDITION 2020

ISBN: 978-93-6589-813-2

LIMITS OF LIABILITY AND DISCLAIMER OF WARRANTY

The Author and Publisher of this book have tried their best to ensure that the programmes, procedures and functions described in the book are correct. However, the author and the publishers make no warranty of any kind, expressed or implied, with regard to these programmes or the documentation contained in the book. The author and publisher shall not be liable in any event of any damages, incidental or consequential, in connection with, or arising out of the furnishing, performance or use of these programmes, procedures and functions. Product name mentioned are used for identification purposes only and may be trademarks of their respective companies.

All trademarks referred to in the book are acknowledged as properties of their respective owners.

Distributors:

BPB PUBLICATIONS
20, Ansari Road, Darya Ganj
New Delhi-110002
Ph: 23254990/23254991

DECCAN AGENCIES
4-3-329, Bank Street,
Hyderabad-500195
Ph: 24756967/24756400

MICRO MEDIA
Shop No. 5, Mahendra Chambers,
150 DN Rd. Next to Capital Cinema,
V.T. (C.S.T.) Station, MUMBAI-400 001
Ph: 22078296/22078297

To View Complete BPB Publications Catalogue Scan the QR Code:

Published by Manish Jain for BPB Publications, 20 Ansari Road, Darya Ganj, New Delhi-110002 and Printed at Akash Press, New Delhi

www.bpbonline.com

Dedicated to

Nalinee & Prabhakar Kanetkar...

About Yashavant Kanetkar

Through his books and online courses on C, C++, Data Structures, VC++, .NET, etc. Yashavant Kanetkar has created, molded and groomed lacs of IT careers in the last three decades. Yashavant's books and online courses have made a significant contribution in creating top-notch IT workforce in India and abroad.

Yashavant's books are globally recognized, and millions of students / professionals have benefited from them. His books have been translated into Hindi, Gujarati, Japanese, Korean, Russian and Chinese languages. Many of his books are published in India, USA, Japan, Singapore, Korea, Russia and China.

Yashavant is a much sought-after speaker in the IT field and has conducted seminars/workshops at TedEx, IITs, NITs, IIITs and global software companies.

Yashavant has been honored with the prestigious "Distinguished Alumnus Award" by IIT Kanpur for his entrepreneurial, professional and academic excellence. This award was given to top 50 alumni of IIT Kanpur who have made significant contributions towards their profession and betterment of society in the last 50 years.

In recognition of his immense contribution to IT education in India, he has been awarded the "Best .NET Technical Contributor" and "Most Valuable Professional" awards by Microsoft for 5 successive years.

Yashavant holds a BE from VJTI Mumbai and M. Tech. from IIT Kanpur. His current affiliations include being the Director of KICIT Pvt. Ltd. He can be reached at kanetkar@kicit.com or through www.ykanetkar.com.

About Aditya Kanetkar

Aditya Kanetkar is currently working as a Software Engineer at Microsoft India Development Center (IDC), Bengaluru. He has 6 years of experience working in the software development industry. His current passion is anything remotely connected to Python, Machine Learning, Distributed Systems, Cloud Computing, Containers and C#. Formerly, he worked at Microsoft HQ, Redmond, Washington and Oracle HQ, Redwood City, California.

Aditya holds a Bachelor's degree in Computer Science and Engineering from IIT Guwahati and a Master's degree in Computer Science from Georgia Tech, Atlanta.

Contents

1 Introduction to Python 1
2 Getting Started 7
3 Python Basics 11
4 Strings 21
5 Decision Control Instruction 29
6 Repetition Control Instruction 43
7 Console Input/Output 55
8 Lists 61
9 Tuples 73
10 Sets 81
11 Dictionaries 89
12 Comprehensions 101
13 Functions 109
14 Recursion 115
15 Functional Programming 125
16 Modules and Packages 131
17 Namespaces 139
18 Classes and Objects 143
19 Intricacies of Classes and Objects 165
20 Containership and Inheritance 173
21 Iterators and Generators 183
22 Exception Handling 191
23 File Input/Output 199
24 Logging 213
25 Miscellany 219
26 Concurrency and Parallelism 229
27 Synchronization 237

28 Numpy Library 245

29 Matplotlib 251

30 Pandas Library 263

31 Security Programming 277

32 Interaction with ChatGPT 281

33 Periodic Tests 289

1 Introduction to Python

Let Us Python Solutions

7th Edition

[A] Answer the following:

(a) Mention 5 fields in which Python is popularly used.

Answer

- System Programming
- Game Programming
- Robotics Programming
- Rapid Prototyping
- Internet Scripting

(b) Where is event-driven programming popularly used?

Answer

Event-driven programming is primarily used for creating GUI application containing elements like windows, check, boxes, button, combo-boxes, scroll-bars, menus etc. When we interact with these GUI elements through mouse/keyboard/touch an event occurs and a function gets called to tackle that event.

(c) Why is Python called portable language?

Answer

We can create and test code on one platform and run it on any other platform. This makes Python a portable language.

(d) What is the single most important feature of different programming models discussed in this chapter?

Answer

Functional programming model - It decomposes a problem into a set of functions.

Procedural programming model - It solves a problem by implementing one statement (procedure) at a time. Thus, it contains explicit steps that are executed in a specific order. It also uses functions, but these are not mathematical functions like the ones used in functional programming. Functional programming focuses on expressions, whereas Procedural programming focuses on statements.

Object-oriented programming model - It mimics the real world by creating inside the computer a mini-world of objects.

Event-driven programming model - It generates events when we interact with different GUI elements like Windows, check boxes, buttons, combo-boxes, scroll bars, menus, etc. Each event is tackled by calling an event handler function.

(e) Which of the following is not a feature of Python?

- Static typing
- Variable declaration before use
- Run-time error handling through error numbers
- Library support for containers like Lists, Dictionaries, Tuples

Answer

- Static typing
- Variable declaration before use
- Run-time error handling through error numbers

(f) Give an example application of each of the following programming models:

- Functional model
- Procedural model
- Object-oriented model
- Event-driven model

Answer

- Functional model: Finding factorial value of a number.
- Procedural model: Step-by-step procedure to sort a set of numbers.
- Object-oriented model: Interaction of objects like customer, product, order, etc.
- Event-driven model: A GUI application which displays "Hi" on left-click of a mouse and "Hello" on right-click of a mouse.

[B] State whether the following statements are True or False:

(a) Python is free to use and distribute.

Answer

True

(b) Same Python program can work on different OS - microprocessor combinations.

Answer

True

(c) It is possible to use C++ or Java libraries in a Python program.

Answer

True

(d) In Python type of the variable is decided based on its usage.

Answer

True

(e) Python cannot be used for building GUI applications.

Answer

False

(f) Python supports functional, procedural, object-oriented and event-driven programming models.

Answer

True

(g) GUI applications are based on event-driven programming model.

Answer

True

(h) Functional programming model consists of interaction of multiple objects.

Answer

False

[C] Match the following:

a. Functional programming	1. GUI element-based interaction
b. Event-driven programming	2. Interaction of objects
c. Procedural programming	3. Statements

d. OOP 4. Math-like functions

Answer

Functional programming - Math-like functions
Event-driven programming - GUI element-based interaction
Procedural programming - Statements
Object-oriented programming - Interaction of objects

[D] Fill in the blanks:

(a) Functional programming paradigm is also known as Declarative programming model.

(b) Procedural programming paradigm is also known as Imperative programming model.

(c) Python was created by Guido Van Rossum.

(d) Python programmers are often called Pythonists or Pythonistas.

2 Getting Started

Let Us Python Solutions

7th Edition

[A] Answer the following questions:

(a) What do the prompts C:\>, $ and >>> signify?

Answer

>>> signifies Python shell prompt.

(b) In which two modes can IDLE be used?

Answer

Interactive mode and Script mode are the two modes used in IDLE.

(c) What is the purpose of the two programming modes offered by IDLE?

Answer

Interactive mode is used for exploring Python syntax, seeking help and debugging short programs. Script mode is used for writing full-fledge Python Programs.

(d) How can third party libraries be used in a Python program?

Answer

2

[B] Match the following pairs:

a. pip	1. Advanced mathematical operations
b. Jupyter	2. Scientific computing
c. Spyder	3. Manipulate numerical tables
d. PyPI	4. Visualization
e. NumPy	5. Computer vision
f. SciPy	6. Package installation tool
g. Pandas	7. Build and document applications
h. MatPlotLib	8. Scientific library
i. OpenCV	9. Python package index

Answer

a. pip	1. Package installation tool
b. Jupyter	2. Build and document applications
c. Spyder	3. Advanced mathematical operation
d. PyPI	4. Python package index

e. NumPy — 5. Scientific library
f. SciPy — 6. Scientific computing
g. Pandas — 7. Manipulate numerical tables
h. MatPlotLib — 8. Visualization
i. OpenCV — 9. Computer vision

[C] State whether the following statements are True or False:

(a) Python is a specification that can be implemented through languages like Python, C#, Java, etc.

Answer

True

(b) CPython is implementation of Python specification, written in C.

Answer

True

(c) Python program is first compiled into byte code, which is then interpreted.

Answer

True

(d) Most Linux distributions already contain Python.

Answer

False

(e) The Windows system does not contain Python and it needs to be separately installed.

Answer

True

(f) Python programs can be built using IDLE, NetBeans, PyCharm and Visual Studio Code.

Answer

True

(g) Third-party Python packages are distributed using PyPI.

Answer

True

3 Python Basics

Let Us Python Solutions

7th Edition

[A] Answer the following:

(a) Write a program that swaps the values of variables **a** and **b**. You are not allowed to use a third variable. You are not allowed to perform arithmetic on **a** and **b**.

Program

```
# Swap values of two variables
a = 5
b = 10
a, b = b, a
print('a =' , a)
print('b =' , b)
```

Output

```
a = 10
b = 5
```

(b) Write a program that makes use of trigonometric functions available in math module.

Program

```
# Use of trigonometric functions
import math
a = math.pi / 6
print('The value of sine of pi / 6 is' , end = ' ')
print(math.sin(a))
print('The value of cosine of pi / 6 is' , end = ' ')
print(math.cos(a))
```

Output

```
The value of sine of pi / 6 is 0.49999999999999994
The value of cosine of pi / 6 is 0.8660254037844387
```

(c) Write a program that generates 5 random numbers in the range 10 to 50. Use a seed value of 6. Make a provision to change this seed value every time you execute the program by associating it with time of execution?

Program

```
# Generate random numbers
import random
import time

random.seed(6)
for i in range(5) :
    print(random.randint(10, 50))

print( )
t = int(time.time( ))
random.seed(t)
for i in range(5) :
    print(random.randint(10, 50))
```

Output

```
46
15
41
26
12

39
36
21
13
18
```

(d) Use **trunc( ), floor( )** and **ceil( )** for numbers -2.8, -0.5, 0.2, 1.5 and 2.9 to understand the difference between these functions clearly.

Program

```
# Use of trunc( ), ceil( ) functions
import math
print(math.floor(-2.8))
print(math.trunc(-2.8))
print(math.ceil(-2.8))
print(math.floor(-0.5))
print(math.trunc(-0.5))
print(math.ceil(-0.5))
```

```
print(math.floor(0.2))
print(math.trunc(0.2))
print(math.ceil(0.2))
print(math.floor(1.5))
print(math.trunc(1.5))
print(math.ceil(1.5))
print(math.floor(2.9))
print(math.trunc(2.9))
print(math.ceil(2.9))
```

Output

```
-3
-2
-2
-1
0
0
0
0
1
1
1
2
2
2
3
```

(e) Assume a suitable value for temperature of a city in Fahrenheit degrees. Write a program to convert this temperature into Centigrade degrees and print both temperatures.

Program

```
farh = 212
cen = ((farh - 32) * 5 / 9)
print(farh, cen)
```

Output

```
212 100.0
```

(f) Given three sides a, b, c of a triangle, write a program to obtain and print the values of three angles rounded to the next integer. Use the formulae:

$a^2 = b^2 + c^2 - 2bc \cos A$, $b^2 = a^2 + c^2 - 2ac \cos B$, $c^2 = a^2 + b^2 - 2ab \cos C$

Program

```
import math
a, b, c = 3, 4, 5
angleA = (math.acos((b * b + c * c - a * a ) / ( 2 * b * c )) * 180) /
3.14
print(angleA)
angleB = (math.acos((a * a + c * c - b * b ) / ( 2 * a * c )) * 180) / 3.14
print(angleB)
angleC = (math.acos((a * a + b * b - c * c ) / ( 2 * a * b )) * 180) /
3.14
print(angleC)
```

Output

```
36.88859859324559
53.157050713468216
90.04564930671381
```

[B] How will you perform the following operations?

(a) Print imaginary part out of 2 + 3j

Answer

```
print(a.imag)
```

(b) Obtain conjugate of 4 + 2j

Answer

```
a = 4 + 2j
b = a.conjugate( )
```

(c) Print decimal equivalent of binary '1100001110'

Answer

```
print(int('1100001110', 2))
```

(d) Convert a float value 4.33 into a numeric string

Answer

a = str(4.33)

(e) Obtain integer quotient and remainder while dividing 29 with 5

Answer

divmod(29, 5)

(f) Obtain hexadecimal equivalent of decimal 34567

Answer

hex(34567)

(g) Round-off 45.6782 to second decimal place

Answer

a = round(45.6782, 2)

(h) Obtain 4 from 3.556

Answer

a = round(3.556)

(i) Obtain 17 from 16.7844

Answer

a = round(16.7844)

(j) Obtain remainder on dividing 3.45 with 1.22

Answer

a = 3.45 % 1.22

[C] Which of the following is invalid variable name and why?

BASICSALARY - Valid

_basic - Valid

basic-hra - Invalid. Cannot contain special character -

#MEAN - Invalid. Cannot start with #

group. - Invalid. Cannot end with .

422 - Invalid. Cannot start with digit

pop in 2020 - Invalid. Cannot contain space

over - Valid

timemindovermatter - Valid

SINGLE - Valid

hELLO - Valid

queue. - Invalid. Cannot end with .

team'svictory - Invalid. Cannot contain special character '

Plot # 3 - Invalid. Cannot contain space and special character #

2015_DDay - Invalid. Cannot start with digit

[D] Evaluate the following expressions:

(a) 2 ** 6 // 8 % 2

Answer

= 64 // 8 % 2
= 8 % 2
= 0

(b) 9 ** 2 // 5 - 3

Answer

= 81 // 5 - 3
= 16 - 3
= 13

(c) 10 + 6 - 2 % 3 + 7 - 2

Answer

= 10 + 6 - 2 + 7 - 2
= 16 - 5 + 7 - 2
= 14 + 7 - 2
= 21 - 2
= 19

(d) 5 % 10 + 10 -23 * 4 // 3

Answer

= 5 + 10 - 23 * 4 // 3
= 5 + 10 - 92 // 3
= 5 + 10 - 30
= 15 - 30
= -15

(e) 5 + 5 // 5 - 5 * 5 ** 5 % 5

Answer

= 5 + 5 // 5 - 5 * 3125 % 5
= 5 + 1 - 5 * 3125 % 5
= 5 + 1 - 15625 % 5
= 5 + 1 - 0
= 6

(f) 7 % 7 + 7 // 7 - 7 * 7

Answer

= 0 + 7 // 7 - 7 * 7
= 0 + 1 - 7 * 7
= 0 + 1 - 49
= 1 - 49
= -48

[E] Evaluate the following expressions:

(a) min(2, 6, 8, 5)

Answer

2

(b) bin(46)

Answer

0b101110

(c) round(10.544336, 2)

Answer

10.54

(d) math.hypot(6, 8)

Answer

10

(e) math.modf(3.1415)

Answer

0.14150000000000018, 3.0

[F] Match the following:

a. complex	1. \
b. Escape special character	2. Container type
c. Tuple	3. Basic type
d. Natural logarithm	4. log( )
e. Common logarithm	5. log10( )

Answer

complex - Basic type
Escape special character - \
Tuple - Container type
Natural Logarithm - log( )
Common logarithm - log10( )

4 Strings

Let Us Python Solutions

7th Edition

[A] Answer the following:

(a) Write a program that generates the following output from the string 'Shenanigan'.

```
S h
a n
enanigan
Shenan
Shenan
Shenan
Shenan
Shenanigan
Seaia
Snin
Saa
ShenaniganType
ShenanWabbite
```

Program

```
# Extract string subparts
s = 'Shenanigan'
print(s[0], s[1])
print(s[4], s[5])
print(s[2:])
print(s[:6])
print(s[:-4])
print(s[-10:-4])
print(s[0:6])
print(s[:])
print(s[0:10:2])
print(s[0:10:3])
print(s[0:10:4])
s = 'Shenanigan'
g = 'Type'
a = s + g
print(a)
s = 'Shenanigan'
t = 'Wabbite'
b = s[:6] + t
print(b)
```

Output

```
S h
a n
enanigan
Shenan
Shenan
Shenan
Shenan
Shenanigan
Seaia
Snin
Saa
ShenaniganType
ShenanWabbite
```

(b) Write a program to convert the following string

'Visit ykanetkar.com for online courses in programming'

into

'Visit Ykanetkar.com For Online Courses In Programming'

Program

```
# Capitalize each word of a string
s = 'Visit ykanetkar.com for online courses in programming'
t = ''
for w in s.split( ) :
    t = t + w.capitalize( ) + ' '
print(t)
```

Output

```
Visit Ykanetkar.com For Online Courses In Programming
```

(c) Write a program to convert the following string

'Light travels faster than sound. This is why some people appear bright until you hear them speak.'

into

'LIGHT travels faster than SOUND. This is why some people appear bright until you hear them speak.'

Program

```
# Search and replace in a string
msg = 'Light travels faster than sound. This is why some people appear bright until you hear them speak.'
newmsg = msg.replace('Light', 'LIGHT').replace('sound', 'SOUND')
print(newmsg)
```

Output

```
LIGHT travels faster than SOUND. This is why some people appear bright until you hear them speak.
```

(d) What will be the output of the following program?

```
s = 'HumptyDumpty'
print('s = ', s)
print(s.isalpha( ))
print(s.isdigit( ))
print(s.isalnum( ))
print(s.islower( ))
print(s.isupper( ))
print(s.startswith('Hump'))
print(s.endswith('Dump'))
```

Output

```
s =  HumptyDumpty
True
False
True
False
False
True
False
```

(e) What is the purpose of a raw string?

Answer

Python raw string is created by prefixing a string literal with 'r' or 'R'. Python raw string treats backslash (\) as a literal character. This is useful when we want to have a string that contains backslash and do not want it to be treated as an escape character.

(f) If we wish to work with an individual word in the following string, how will you separate them out:

'The difference between stupidity and genius is that genius has its limits'

Program

```
msg = 'The difference between stupidity and genius is that genius
has its limits'
for word in msg.split( ) :
    print(word)
```

Output

```
The
difference
between
stupidity
and
genius
is
that
genius
has
its
limits
```

(g) Mention two ways to store a string: He said, "Let Us Python".

Answer

```
s1 = "He said, \"Let Us Python\""
s2 = r'He said, "Let Us Python"'
```

(h) What will be the output of the following code snippet?

```
print(id('Imaginary'))
print(type('Imaginary'))
```

Answer

```
36339048
<class 'str'>
```

(i) What will be the output of the following code snippet?

```
s3 = 'C:\\Users\\Kanetkar\\Documents'
print(s3.split('\\'))
print(s3.partition('\\'))
```

Answer

```
['C:', 'Users', 'Kanetkar', 'Documents']
('C:', '\\', 'Users\\Kanetkar\\Documents')
```

(j) Strings in Python are iterable, sliceable and immutable. (True/False)

Answer

True

(k) How will you extract ' TraPoete' from the string 'ThreadProperties'?

Answer

```
s = 'ThreadProperties'
print(s[::2])
```

(l) How will you eliminate spaces on either side of the string

' Flanked by spaces on either side '?

Answer

```
s = '    Flanked by spaces on either side      '
print(s.strip( ))
```

(m) What will be the output of the following code snippet?

```
s1 = s2 = s3 = "Hello"
print(id(s1), id(s2), id(s3))
```

Answer

36330016 36330016 36330016

(n) What will get stored in **ch in** the following code snippet:

msg = 'Aeroplane'
ch = msg[-0]

Answer

A

[B] Match the following assuming msg = 'Keep yourself warm'

a. msg.partition(' ')	1. 18
b. msg.split(' ')	2. kEEP YOURSELF WARM
c. msg.startswith('Keep')	3. Keep yourself warm
d. msg.endswith('Keep')	4. 3
e. msg.swapcase( )	5. True
f. msg.capitalize( )	6. False
g. msg.count('e')	7. ['Keep', 'yourself', 'warm']
h. len(msg)	8. ('Keep', ' ', 'yourself warm')
i. msg[0]	9. Keep yourself w
j. msg[-1]	10. keep yourself wa
k. msg[1:1:1]	11. K
l. msg[-1:3]	12. empty string
m. msg[:-3]	13. m
n. msg[-3:]	14. arm
o. msg[0:-2]	15. empty string

Answer

msg.partition(' ') - ['Keep','','yourself warm']
msg.split(' ') - ['Keep', 'yourself', 'warm']
msg.startswith('Keep') - True
msg.endswith('Keep') - False
msg.swapcase( ) - kEEP YOURSELF WARM
msg.capitalize( ) - Keep yourself warm
msg.count('e') - 3
len(msg) - 18
msg[0] - K
msg[-1] - m

msg[1:1:1] - empty string
msg[-1:3] - empty string
msg[:-3] - Keep yourself w
msg[-3:] - arm
msg[0:-2] - Keep yourself wa

[C] Give an example string which will return a match for the following regular expressions:

\w+
\d{2}
\w{1,}
\w{2,4}
A*B
\d+?

Answer

01
smiling
1234
AAAAB
1 in 12345

5 Decision Control Instruction

Let Us Python Solutions

7th Edition

[A] Answer the following:

(a) Write conditional expressions for

- If a < 10 b = 20, else b = 30
- Print 'Morning' if time < 12, otherwise print 'Afternoon'
- If marks >= 70, set remarks to True, otherwise False

Answer

```
b = 20 if a < 10 else 30
print('Morning')if time < 12 else print('Afternoon')
remarks = 'True' if marks >= 70 else 'False'
```

(b) Rewrite the following code snippet in 1 line:

```
x = 3
y = 3.0
if x == y :
    print('x and y are equal')
else :
    print('x and y are not equal')
```

Answer

```
x, y = 3, 3.0
print('x and y are equal') if x == y else print('x and y are not equal')
```

Output

```
x and y are equal
```

(c) What happens when a **pass** statement is executed?

Answer

pass statement is a no-op instruction, and nothing happens when it gets executed.

[B] What will be the output of the following programs?

(a)
```
i, j, k = 4, -1, 0
w = i or j or k
x = i and j and k
y = i or j and k
```

```
z = i and j or k
print(w, x, y, z)
```

Output

```
4 0 4 -1
```

(b)
```
a = 10
a = not not a
print(a)
```

Output

```
True
```

(c)
```
x, y, z = 20, 40, 45
if x > y and x > z :
    print('biggest = ' + str(x))
elif y > x and y > z :
    print('biggest = ' + str(y))
elif z > x and z > y :
    print('biggest = ' + str(z))
```

Output

```
biggest = 45
```

(d)
```
num = 30
k = 100 if num <= 10 else 500
print(k)
```

Output

```
500
```

(e)
```
a = 10
b = 60
if a and b > 20 :
    print('Hello')
else :
    print('Hi')
```

Output

```
Hello
```

(f)
```
a = 10
b = 60
if a > 20 and b > 20 :
    print('Hello')
else :
    print('Hi')
```

Output

Hi

(g)
```
a = 10
if a = 30 or 40 or 60 :
    print('Hello')
else :
    print('Hi')
```

Output

Error

(h)
```
a = 10
if a = 30 or a == 40 or a == 60 :
    print('Hello')
else :
    print('Hi')
```

Output

Error

(i)
```
a = 10
if a in (30,  40,  50) :
    print('Hello')
else :
    print('Hi')
```

Output

Hi

[C] Point out the errors, if any, in the following programs:

(a)
```
a = 12.25
b = 12.52
```

```
if a = b :
    print('a and b are equal')
```

Answer

Error: Invalid syntax. Use a == b

(b)
```
if ord('X') < ord('x')
    print('Unicode value of X is smaller than that of x')
```

Answer

Error: Invalid syntax. Use : at the end of if as shown below:
if ord('X') < ord('x') :

(c)
```
x = 10
if x >= 2 then
    print('x')
```

Answer

Error: Invalid syntax. Use : at the end of if as shown below:
if x >= 2 :

(d)
```
x = 10 ; y = 15
if x % 2 = y % 3
    print('Carpathians\n')
```

Answer

Error: Invalid syntax. Use == in place of = during comparison

(e)
```
x, y = 30, 40
if x == y :
    print('x is equal to y')
elseif x > y :
    print('x is greater than y')
elseif x < y :
    print('x is less than y')
```

Answer

Error: Invalid syntax. Use **elif** in place of **elseif**

[D] If a = 10, b = 12, c = 0, find the values of the following expressions:

a != 6 and b > 5
a == 9 or b < 3

```
not ( a < 10 )
not ( a > 5 and c )
5 and c != 8 or c
```

Answer

```
True
False
True
True
True
```

[E] Attempt the following:

(a) Any integer is input through the keyboard. Write a program to find out whether it is an odd number or even number.

Program

```
# Determine whether number is odd or even
x = int(input('Enter any number: '))
j = 2
if x % j == 0 :
   print('Even Number')
else :
   print('Odd Number')
```

Output

```
Enter any number: 48
Even Number
```

(b) Any year is input through the keyboard. Write a program to determine whether the year is a leap year or not.

Program

```
# Determine whether year is leap or not
year = int(input('Enter a year: '))
if year % 4 == 0 :
   if year % 100 == 0 :
      if year % 400 == 0 :
         print(year, 'is a Leap Year')
      else :
         print(year, 'is not a Leap Year')
```

```
    else :
        print(year, 'is a Leap Year')
else :
    print(year, 'is not a Leap Year')
```

Output

```
Enter a year: 1996
1996 is a Leap Year

Enter a year: 2000
2000 is a Leap Year

Enter a year: 1900
1900 is not a Leap Year
```

(c) If ages of Ram, Shyam and Ajay are input through the keyboard, write a program to determine the youngest of the three.

Program

```
# Determine youngest out of three persons
ram_age = int(input('Enter Ram\'s age: '))
shyam_age = int(input('Enter Shyam\'s age: '))
ajay_age = int(input('Enter Ajay\'s age: '))
if ram_age < shyam_age and ram_age < ajay_age :
        print('Youngest is Ram')
elif shyam_age < ram_age and shyam_age < ajay_age :
        print('Youngest is Shyam')
elif ajay_age < ram_age and ajay_age < shyam_age :
       print('Youngest is Ajay')
```

Output

```
Enter Ram's age: 23
Enter Shyam's age: 45
Enter Ajay's age: 34
Youngest is Ram
```

(d) Write a program to check whether a triangle is valid or not, when the three angles of the triangle are entered through the keyboard. A triangle is valid if the sum of all the three angles is equal to 180 degrees.

Program

```
# Determine whether triangle is valid or not
x = int(input('Enter angle no. 1: '))
y = int(input('Enter angle no. 2: '))
z = int(input('Enter angle no. 3: '))
sum_of_angles = x + y + z
if sum_of_angles == 180 :
    print('Valid Triangle')
else :
    print('Is not a Valid Triangle')
```

Output

```
Enter angle no. 1: 45
Enter angle no. 2: 45
Enter angle no. 3: 90
Valid Triangle
```

(e) Write a program to find the absolute value of a number entered through the keyboard.

Program

```
# Obtain absolute value of a number
x = int(input('Enter any number: '))
if x < 0 :
    y = x * (-1)
else :
    y = x
print('Absolute value of', x, 'is', y)
```

Output

```
Enter any number: -20
Absolute value of -20 is 20

Enter any number: 23
Absolute value of 23 is 23
```

(f) Given the length and breadth of a rectangle, write a program to find whether the area of the rectangle is greater than its perimeter. For example, the area of the rectangle with length = 5 and breadth = 4 is greater than its perimeter.

Program

```
# Determine whether area of rectangle is greater than its perimeter
length = int(input('Enter length of rectangle: '))
breadth = int(input('Enter breadth of rectangle: '))

area = length * breadth
perimeter = 2 * (length + breadth)
print('Area =', area, 'Perimeter =', perimeter)
if area > perimeter :
    print('Area of Rectangle is greater than perimeter')
else :
    print('Perimeter of Rectangle is greater than area')
```

Output

```
Enter length of rectangle: 4
Enter breadth of rectangle: 5
Area = 20 Perimeter = 18
Area of Rectangle is greater than perimeter

Enter length of rectangle: 2
Enter breadth of rectangle: 1
Area = 2 Perimeter = 6
Perimeter of Rectangle is greater than area
```

(g) Given three points **(x1, y1)**, **(x2, y2)** and **(x3, y3)**, write a program to check if all the three points fall on one straight line.

Program

```
# Determine whether 3 points are collinear
x1 = int(input('Enter the co-ordinate of x1: '))
y1 = int(input('Enter the co-ordinate of y1: '))
x2 = int(input('Enter the co-ordinate of x2: '))
y2 = int(input('Enter the co-ordinate of y2: '))
x3 = int(input('Enter the co-ordinate of x3: '))
y3 = int(input('Enter the co-ordinate of y3: '))

if x1 == x2 and x2 == x3 :
    print('Collinear')
elif x1 != x2 and x2 != x3 and x3 != x1 :
    # Calculate Slope of line between each pair of points
```

```
s1 = (float(abs(y2 - y1))) / (float(abs(x2 - x1)))
s2 = (float(abs(y3 - y2))) / (float(abs(x3 - x2)))
s3 = (float(abs(y3 - y1))) / (float(abs(x3 - x1)))

if s1 == s2 and s2 == s3 :
    print('Collinear')
else :
    print('Non Collinear')
```

Output

```
Enter the co-ordinate of x1: 4
Enter the co-ordinate of y1: 4
Enter the co-ordinate of x2: 5
Enter the co-ordinate of y2: 5
Enter the co-ordinate of x3: 6
Enter the co-ordinate of y3: 6
All the 3 points lies on the one straight line
```

(h) Given the coordinates **(x, y)** of the center of a circle and its radius, write a program that will determine whether a point lies inside the circle, on the circle or outside the circle. (Hint: Use **sqrt( )** function)

Program

```
# Determine whether point lies inside, outside or on the circle
import math

centerX = int(input('Enter X coord. of center of circle: ' ))
centerY = int(input('Enter Y coord. of center of circle: ' ))

radius = int(input('Enter radius of circle: '))

print('Enter coordinates of point:')
pointX = int(input('Enter X coord. of point: '))
pointY = int(input('Enter Y coord. of point: '))

xDiff = centerX - pointX ;
yDiff = centerY - pointY ;

distance = math.sqrt((xDiff * xDiff) + (yDiff * yDiff))
```

```
if distance == radius :
    print('Point is on the circle')
elif distance < radius :
    print('Point lies inside the circle')
else :
    print('Point lies outside the circle')
```

Output

```
Enter X coord. of center of circle: 0
Enter Y coord. of center of circle: 0
Enter radius of circle: 5
Enter coordinates of point:
Enter X coord. of point: 5
Enter Y coord. of point: 0
Point is on the circle
```

(i) Given a point **(x, y)**, write a program to find out if it lies on the X-axis, Y-axis or on the origin.

Program

```
# Determine where a point lies in coordinate system
x = int(input('Enter X Coord of the point:'))
y = int(input('Enter Y coord of the point:'))

if x == 0 and y == 0 :
    print('Point is the origin')
elif x == 0 and y != 0 :
    print('Point lies on the Y axis')
elif x != 0 and y == 0 :
    print('Point lies on the X axis')
else :
    if x > 0 and y > 0 :
        print('Point lies in the First Quadrant')
    elif x < 0 and y > 0 :
        print('Point lies in the Second Quadrant')
    elif x < 0 and y < 0 :
        print('Point lies in the Third Quadrant')
    else :
        print('Point lies in the Fourth Quadrant')
```

Output

```
Enter X Coord of the point:0
Enter Y coord of the point:0
Point is the origin

Enter X Coord of the point:-10
Enter Y coord of the point:-20
Point lies in the Third Quadrant
```

(j) A year is entered through the keyboard, write a program to determine whether the year is leap or not. Use logical operators **and** and **or**.

Program

```
# Determine whether year is leap or not
year = int(input('Enter a year: '))
if (year % 4 == 0 and year % 100 != 0) or year % 400 == 0 :
    print(year, 'is a leap year')
else :
    print(year, 'is not a leap year')
```

Output

```
Enter a year: 2016
2016 is a Leap Year
```

(k) If the three sides of a triangle are entered through the keyboard, write a program to check whether the triangle is valid or not. The triangle is valid if the sum of two sides is greater than the largest of the three sides.

Program

```
# Determine whether triangle is valid or not
s1 = int(input('Enter the 1st side of triangle: '))
s2 = int(input('Enter the 2nd side of triangle: '))
s3 = int(input('Enter the 3rd side of triangle: '))
if s1 + s2 <= s3 or s2 + s3 <= s1 or s1 + s3 <= s2 :
    print('Invalid Triangle')
else :
    print('Valid Triangle')
```

Output

```
Enter the 1st side of triangle: 6
Enter the 2nd side of triangle: 7
Enter the 3rd side of triangle: 10
Valid Triangle.

Enter the 1st side of triangle: 5
Enter the 2nd side of triangle: 3
Enter the 3rd side of triangle: 12
Invalid Triangle
```

(l) If the three sides of a triangle are entered through the keyboard, write a program to check whether the triangle is isosceles, equilateral, scalene or right-angled triangle.

Program

```
# Determine the type of triangle
s1 = int(input('Enter the 1st side of triangle: '))
s2 = int(input('Enter the 2nd side of triangle: '))
s3 = int(input('Enter the 3rd side of triangle: '))

if s1 + s2 <= s3 or s2 + s3 <= s1 or s1 + s3 <= s2 :
    print('The sides do not form a triangle')
else :
    if s1 != s2 and s2 != s3 and s3 != s1 :
        print('Scalene triangle')

    if s1 == s2 and s2 != s3 :
        print('Isosceles triangle')

    if s2 == s3 and s3 != s1 :
        print('Isosceles triangle')

    if s1 == s3 and s3 != s2 :
        print('Isosceles triangle')

    if s1 == s2 and s2 == s3 :
        print('Equilateral triangle')

    a = ( s1 * s1) == ( s2 * s2) + ( s3 * s3)
    b = ( s2 * s2) == ( s1 * s1) + ( s3 * s3)
    c = ( s3 * s3) == ( s1 * s1) + ( s2 * s2)
```

```
    if a or b or c :
        print('Right-angled triangle')
```

Output

```
Enter the 1st side of triangle: 6
Enter the 2nd side of triangle: 8
Enter the 3rd side of triangle: 10
Scalene triangle
Right-angled triangle

Enter the 1st side of triangle: 3
Enter the 2nd side of triangle: 3
Enter the 3rd side of triangle: 3
Equilateral triangle

Enter the 1st side of triangle: 5
Enter the 2nd side of triangle: 3
Enter the 3rd side of triangle: 12
The sides do not form a triangle
```

6

Repetition Control Instruction

Let Us Python Solutions

7th Edition

[A] Answer the following:

(a) When does the **else** block of a **while** loop go to work?

Answer

Else block is optional. If present, it is executed when condition fails.

(b) Can **range( )** function be used to generate numbers from 0.1 to 1.0 in steps of 0.1?

Answer

No. **range( )** function cannot generate float numbers.

(c) Can a **while** loop be nested within a **for** loop and vice versa?

Answer

Yes, a **while** loop can be nested within a **for** loop and vice versa.

(d) Can a **while/for** loop be used in an **if/else** and vice versa?

Answer

Yes, a **while/for** loop be used in an **if/else** and vice versa.

(e) Can a do-while loop be used to repeat a set of statements?

Answer

There is no **do-while** loop in Python.

(f) How will you write an equivalent **for** loop for the following?

```
count = 1
while count <= 10 :
    print(count)
    count = count + 1
```

Answer

```
for count in range(1, 11) :
   print(count)
```

(g) What will be the output of the following code snippet?

```
for index in range(20, 10, -3) :
```

```
print(index, end = ' ')
```

Answer

20 17 14 11

(h) Why should **break** and **continue** be always used with an **if** embedded in a **while** or **for** loop?

Answer

If used without **if**, **break** would terminate the loop during first iteration itself.

If **continue** is used without **if**, the statements below it would never get executed.

[B] Point out the errors, if any, in the following programs:

(a)
```
j = 1
while j <= 10 :
    print(j)
    j++
```

Answer

Error. We cannot increment **j** using **j++**, as there is no incrementation operator in Python. Instead, use either **j = j + 1** or **j += 1**.

(b)
```
while true :
    print('Infinite loop')
```

Answer

Error. Use **True** instead of **true**.

(c)
```
lst = [10, 20, 30,  40, 50]
for count = 1 to 5 :
    print(lst[ i ])
```

Answer

Error. Wrong usage of **for** loop. We should have used:

```
for num in lst :
    print(num)
```

(d)
```
i = 15
not while i < 10 :
    print(i)
    i -= 1
```

Answer

Error. Improper use of **while**. We should have used:

while i >= 10 :

(e)
```
# Print alphabets from A to Z
for alpha in range(65, 91) :
    print(ord(alpha), end=' ')
```

Answer

Error. Instead of **ord( )** use **chr( )** function to print character corresponding to ASCII value.

(f)
```
for i in range(0.1, 1.0, 0.25) :
    print(i)
```

Answer

Error. **range( )** function cannot be used to generate a sequence of floats.

(g)
```
i = 1
while i <= 10 :
    j = 1
    while j <= 5 :
        print(i, j )
        j += 1
        break
    print(i, j)
    i += 1
```

Answer

No error.

[C] Match the following pairs for the values each **range( )** function will generated when used in a **for** loop.

a. range(5) 1. 1, 2, 3, 4

b. range(1, 10, 3)
c. range(10, 1, -2)
d. range(1, 5)
e. range(-2)

2. 0, 1, 2, 3, 4
3. Nothing
4. 10, 8, 6, 4, 2
5. 1, 4, 7

Answer

range(5) - 0, 1, 2, 3, 4
range(1, 10, 3) - 1, 4, 7
range(10, 1, -2) - 10, 8, 6, 4, 2
range(1, 5) - 1, 2, 3, 4, 5
range(-2) - Nothing

[D] Attempt the following:

(a) Write a program to print first 25 odd numbers using **range( )**.

Program

```
# Generate first 25 odd numbers
j = 1
print('First 25 Odd Numbers:')
for i in range(50) :
    if i % j == 1 :
        print(i, end = ', ')
    i += 1
```

Output

First 25 Odd Numbers:
1, 3, 5, 7, 9, 11, 13, 15, 17, 19, 21, 23, 25, 27, 29, 31, 33, 35, 37, 39, 41, 43, 45, 47, 49,

(b) Rewrite the following program using for loop.

```
lst = ['desert', 'dessert', 'to', 'too', 'lose', 'loose']
s = 'Mumbai'
i = 0
while i < len(lst) :
    if i > 3 :
        break
    else :
        print(i, lst[i], s[i])
        i += 1
```

Program

```
# Rewrite using for loop
lst = ['desert','dessert','to','too','lose','loose']
s = 'Mumbai'
i = 0
for i, ele in enumerate(lst) :
    if i > 3 :
        break
    print(i, ele, s[i])
```

Output

```
0 desert M
1 dessert u
2 to m
3 too b
```

(c) Write a program to count the number of alphabets and number of digits in the string 'Nagpur-440010'.

Program

```
# Count alphabets, digits and special symbols in a string
string = 'Nagpur-440010'
alphabets = digits = special = 0

for i in range(len(string)) :
    if(string[i].isalpha( )) :
        alphabets = alphabets + 1
    elif(string[i].isdigit( )) :
        digits = digits + 1
    else :
        special = special + 1

print('Number of Alphabets =', alphabets)
print('Number of Digits =', digits)
print('Number of Special Characters =', special)
```

Output

```
Number of Alphabets = 6
```

Number of Digits = 6
Number of Special Characters = 1

(d) A five-digit number is entered through the keyboard. Write a program to obtain the reversed number and to determine whether the original and reversed numbers are equal or not.

Program

```
# Reverse a 5-digit number and compare with original
num = int(input('Enter a 5-digit number: '))
orinum = num
revnum = 0
while(num > 0) :
    rem = num % 10
    revnum = (revnum * 10) + rem
    num = num // 10

print('Original number =', orinum)
print('Reversed number = ', revnum)
if orinum == revnum :
    print('Original and reversed numbers are same')
else :
    print('Original and reversed numbers are different')
```

Output

```
Enter a 5-digit number: 12345
Original number = 12345
Reversed number =  54321
Original and reversed number are different

Enter a 5-digit number: 12221
Original number = 12221
Reversed number =  12221
Original and reversed numbers are same
```

(e) Write a program to find the factorial value of any number entered through the keyboard.

Program

```
number = int(input('Enter a number: '))
```

```
fact = 1
for i in range(1, number + 1) :
    fact = fact * i
print('Factorial value = ', fact)
```

Output

```
Enter a number: 5
Factorial value =  120
```

(f) Write a program to print out all Armstrong numbers between 100 and 500. If sum of cubes of each digit of the number is equal to the number itself, then the number is called an Armstrong number. For example, 153 = (1 * 1 * 1) + (5 * 5 * 5) + (3 * 3 * 3).

Program

```
print('Armstrong numbers between 1 and 500 are:')
for num in range(100, 501) :
    n = num
    d3 = n % 10
    n = int(n / 10)
    d2 = n % 10
    n = int(n / 10)
    d1 = n % 10
    if d1 * d1 * d1 + d2 * d2 * d2 + d3 * d3 * d3 == num :
        print(num)
```

Output

```
Armstrong numbers between 100 and 500 are:
153
370
371
407
```

(g) Write a program to print all prime numbers from 1 to 300.

Program

```
lower = 1
upper = 300
print('All Prime numbers from 1 to 300:')
for num in range(lower, upper + 1) :
```

```
    for n in range(2, num) :
        if (num % n) == 0 :
            break
    else :
        print(num, end = ', ')
```

Output

```
All Prime numbers from 1 to 300:
1, 2, 3, 5, 7, 11, 13, 17, 19, 23, 29, 31, 37, 41, 43, 47, 53, 59, 61, 67,
71, 73, 79, 83, 89, 97, 101, 103, 107, 109, 113, 127, 131, 137, 139,
149, 151, 157, 163, 167, 173, 179, 181, 191, 193, 197, 199, 211,
223, 227, 229, 233, 239, 241, 251, 257, 263, 269, 271, 277, 281,
283, 293,
```

(h) Write a program to print the multiplication table of the number entered by the user. The table should be displayed in the following form:

```
29 * 1 = 29
29 * 2 = 58
...
```

Program

```
num = int(input('Enter any number: '))
lower = 1
upper = 10
for i in range(lower, upper + 1) :
    print(num, 'x', i , '=' , num * i)
```

Output

```
Enter any number: 29
29 x 1 = 29
29 x 2 = 58
29 x 3 = 87
29 x 4 = 116
29 x 5 = 145
29 x 6 = 174
29 x 7 = 203
29 x 8 = 232
29 x 9 = 261
29 x 10 = 290
```

(i) When interest compounds **q** times per year at an annual rate of **r** % for **n** years, the principal **p** compounds to an amount **a** as per the following formula:

$a = p (1 + r / q)^{nq}$

Write a program to read 10 sets of **p, r, n** & **q** and calculate the corresponding **a**s.

Program

```
for i in range(10) :
    p = float(input('Enter value of p: '))
    r = float(input('Enter value of r: '))
    n = float(input('Enter value of n: '))
    q = float(input('Enter value of q: '))
    a = p * ((1 + r / 100 / q) ** (n * q))
    print('Compound Interest = Rs.', a)
```

Output

```
Enter value of p: 1000
Enter value of r: 5
Enter value of n: 3
Enter value of q: 4
Compound Interest = Rs. 1160.7545177229981
...
```

(j) Write a program to generate all Pythagorean Triplets with side lengths less than or equal to 30.

Program

```
n = 31
for i in range(1, n) :
    for j in range((i + 1), (n + 1), 1) :
        t = (i * i) + (j * j)
        for k in range((i + 2), (n + 1), 1) :
            if (t == k * k) :
                print(i , j, k)
```

Output

```
3 4 5
5 12 13
6 8 10
7 24 25
8 15 17
9 12 15
10 24 26
12 16 20
15 20 25
18 24 30
20 21 29
```

(k) The population of a town today is 100000. The population has increased steadily at the rate of 10 % per year for the last 10 years. Write a program to determine the population at the end of each year in the last decade.

Program

```
population = 100000
for i in range(10) :
    population += int(population * 10 / 100)
    print('Year', i + 1, ':', population)
```

Output

```
Year 1 : 110000
Year 2 : 121000
Year 3 : 133100
Year 4 : 146410
Year 5 : 161051
Year 6 : 177156
Year 7 : 194871
Year 8 : 214358
Year 9 : 235793
Year 10 : 259372
```

(l) Ramanujan number is the smallest number that can be expressed as sum of two cubes in two different ways. Write a program to print all such numbers up to a reasonable limit.

Program

```
print('Ramanujan Numbers:')
for i in range(1, 31):
    for j in range(1, 31):
        for k in range(1, 31):
            for l in range(1, 31):
                if (i != j and i != k and i != l) and (j != k and j != l)
                                 and (k != l ) :
                    if i * i * i + j * j * j == k * k * k + l * l * l :
                        print(i, j, k, l)
```

Output

```
Ramanujan Numbers:
1    12    9    10
1    12    10    9
2    16    9    15
.. .. .. .. .. ..
```

(m) Write a program to print 24 hours of day with suitable suffixes like AM, PM, Noon and Midnight.

Program

```
for hour in range(24) :
    if hour == 0 :
        print('12 Midnight')
        continue
    if hour < 12 :
        print(hour, 'AM')
    if hour == 12 :
        print('12 Noon')
    if hour > 12 :
        print(hour % 12, 'PM')
```

Output

```
12 Midnight
1 AM
2 AM
.. ..
```

7 Console Input Output

Let Us Python Solutions 7th Edition

[A] Attempt the following:

(a) How will you make the following code more compact?

```
print('Enter ages of 3 persons')
age1 = input( )
age2 = input( )
age3 = input( )
```

Answer

```
age1, age2, age3 = input('Enter 3 values: ').split(',')
```

(b) How will you print "Rendezvous" in a line and retain the cursor in the same line in which the output has been printed?

Answer

```
print('Rendezvous', end = '')
```

(c) What will be the output of the following code snippet?

```
l, b = 1.5678, 10.5
print('length = {l} breadth = {b}')
```

Output

```
length = {l} breadth = {b}
```

(d) In the following statement what do > 5, > 7 and > 8 signify?

```
print(f'{n:>5}{n ** 2:>7}{n ** 3:>8}')
```

Output

n > 5 indicates that the value of **n** is printed right-justified in 5 columns. Similarly, n ** 2:>7 indicates that the value of **n ** 2** is printed right-justified within 7 columns.

(e) What will be the output of the following code segment?

```
name = 'Sanjay'
cellno = 9823017892
print(f'{name:15} : {cellno:10}')
```

Output

Sanjay   : 9823017892

(f) How will you print the output of the following code segment using fstring?

```
x, y, z =10, 20, 40
print('{0:<5}{1:<7}{2:<8}'.format(x, y, z))
```

Output

```
print(f'{x:<5}{y:<7}{z:<8}')
```

(g) How will you receive an arbitrary number of floats from keyboard?

Output

```
numbers = [float(x) for x in input('Enter values: ').split( )]
for n in numbers :
    print(n + 10)
```

(h) What changes should be made in

```
print(f'{'\nx = ':4}{x:>10}{'\ny = ':4}{y:>10}')
```

to produce the output given below:

```
x =      14.99
y =     114.39
```

Output

```
print(f'{x = :>10}\n{y = :>10}')
```

(i) How will you receive a boolean value as input?

Output

```
b = bool(input('Enter boolean value: '))
```

(j) How will you receive a complex number as input?

Output

```
c = complex(input('Enter complex value: '))
```

(k) How will you display **price** in 10 columns with 4 places beyond decimal points? Assume value of price to be 1.5567894.

Output

```
price = 1.5567894
print(f'{price =:10.4}')
```

(l) Write a program to receive an arbitrary number of floats using one **input( )** statement. Calculate the average of floats received.

Program

```
# Receive arbitrary number of floats
num = int(input('How many numbers do you wish to input: '))
totalsum = 0
number = [float(x) for x in input('Enter all numbers: ').split( )]
for n in range(len(number)) :
    totalsum = totalsum + number[n]
avg = totalsum / num
print('Average of', num, 'numbers is:', avg)
```

Output

```
How many numbers do you wish to input: 5
Enter all numbers: 10 20 30 40 50
Average of 5 numbers is: 30.0
```

(m) Write a program to receive the following using one **input( )** statement.

Name of the person
Years of service
Diwali bonus received

Calculate and print the agreement deduction as per the following formula:

deduction = 2 * years of service + bonus * 5.5 / 100

Program

```
data = input('Name, year of service, diwali bonus: ').split(',')
name = data[0]
yos = int(data[1])
```

```
bonus = float(data[2])
deduction = float((2 * yos + bonus * 5.5 ) / 100)
print('Deduction = Rs.', deduction)
```

Output

```
Name, year of service, diwali bonus: Ramesh, 3, 9500
Deduction = Rs. 522.56
```

(n) Which import statement should be added to use the built-in functions **input( )** and **print( )**?

Answer

No import statement is needed to use **input( )** and **print( )** as they are global functions which are available everywhere..

(o) Is the following statement correct?

```
print('Result = ' + 4 > 3)
```

Answer

No. String cannot be concatenated with a boolean value. The correct form would be:

```
print('Result = ' + str(4 > 3))
```

(p) Write a program to print the values

a = 12.34, b = 234.39, c = 444.34, d = 1.23, e = 34.67

as shown below:

```
a =      12.34
b =     234.39
c =     444.34
d =       1.23
e =      34.67
```

Program

```
a, b, c, d, e = 12.34, 234.39, 444.34, 1.23, 34.67
print(f'a = {a:>10}')
print(f'b = {b:>10}')
print(f'c = {c:>10}')
```

```
print(f'd = {d:>10}')
print(f'e = {e:>10}')
```

Output

```
a =      12.34
b =     234.39
c =     444.34
d =       1.23
e =      34.67
```

[B] Match the following:

a. Default value of sep in print( ) 1. ' '
b. Default value of end in print( ) 2. Using fstring
c. Easiest way to print output 3. Right justify num in 5 columns
d. Return type of split( ) 4. Left justify num in 5 columns
e. print('{num:>5}') 5. str
f. print('{num:<5}') 6. \n

Answer

Default value of sep in print( ) - ' '
Default value of end in print( ) - \n
Easiest way to print output - Using fstring
Return type of split( ) - str
print('{num:>5}') - Right justify num in 5 columns
print('{num:<5}') - Left justify num in 5 columns

8 Lists

Let Us Python Solutions

7th Edition

[A] What will be the output of the following programs?

(a)
```
msg = list('www.kicit.com')
ch = msg[-1]
print(ch)
```

Answer

```
m
```

(b)
```
msg = list('kanlabs.teachable.com')
s = msg[4:6]
print(s)
```

Answer

```
['a', 'b']
```

(c)
```
msg = 'Online Courses - KanLabs'
s = list(msg[:3])
print(s)
```

Answer

```
['O', 'n', 'l']
```

(d)
```
msg = 'Rahate Colony'
s = list(msg[-5:-2])
print(s)
```

Answer

```
['o', 'l', 'o']
```

(e)
```
s = list('KanLabs')
t = s[::-1]
print(t)
```

Answer

```
['s', 'b', 'a', 'L', 'n', 'a', 'K']
```

(f)
```
num1 = [10, 20, 30, 40, 50]
num2 = num1
print(id(num1))
print(type(num2))
print(isinstance(num1, list))
```

```
print(num1 is num2)
```

Answer

```
40423528
<class 'list'>
True
True
```

(g)

```
num = [10, 20, 30, 40, 50]
num[2:4] = [ ]
print(num)
```

Answer

```
[10, 20, 50]
```

(h)

```
num1 = [10, 20, 30, 40, 50]
num2 = [60, 70, 80]
num1.append(num2)
print(num1)
```

Answer

```
[10, 20, 30, 40, 50, [60, 70, 80]]
```

(i)

```
lst = [10, 25, 4, 12, 3, 8]
sorted(lst)
print(lst)
```

Answer

```
[10, 25, 4, 12, 3, 8]
```

(j)

```
a = [1, 2, 3, 4]
b = [1, 2, 5]
print(a < b)
```

Answer

```
True
```

[B] Attempt the following questions:

(a) Which of the following is a valid List?

['List'] {"List"} ("List") "List"

Answer

```
['List']
```

(b) What will happen on execution of the following code snippet?

```
s = list('Hello')
s[1] = 'M'
```

Answer

The element 'e' in the list s would be replaced by 'M'.

(c) The following code snippet deletes elements 30 and 40 from the list:

```
num = [10, 20, 30, 40, 50]
del(num[2:4])
```

In which other way can the same effect be obtained?

Answer

```
num[2:4] = [ ]
```

(d) Which of the following is an INCORRECT list?

```
a = [0, 1, 2, 3, [10, 20, 30]]
a = [10, 'Suraj', 34555.50]
a = [[10, 20, 30], [40, 50, 60]]
```

Answer

None. All lists are correct. A list can contain dissimilar elements.

(e) From the list given below

```
num1 = [10, 20, 30, 40, 50]
```

How will you create a list **num2** containing:

['A', 'B', 'C', 10, 20, 30, 40, 50, 'Y', 'Z']

Answer

```
num1 = [10, 20, 30, 40, 50]
num2 = ['A', 'B', 'C', *num1, 'Y', 'Z']
```

(f) Given a list

lst = [10, 25, 4, 12, 3, 8]

How will you sort it in descending order?

Answer

lst.sort(reverse = True)

(g) Given a list

lst = [10, 25, 4, 12, 3, 8]

How will you check whether 30 is present in the list or not?

Answer

print(30 in lst)

(h) Given a list

lst = [10, 25, 4, 12, 3, 8]

How will you insert 30 between 25 and 4?

Answer

lst.insert(2, 30)

(i) Given a string

s = 'Hello'

How will you obtain a list ['H', 'e', 'l', 'l', 'o'] from it?

Answer

lst = list(s)

[C] Answer the following:

(a) Write a program to create a list of 5 odd integers. Replace the third element with a list of 4 even integers. Flatten, sort and print the list.

Program

```
# Modify, flatten and sort list
x = [1, 3, 5, 7, 9]
```

```
y = [2, 4, 6, 8]
x[2] = y
print(x)
x = x[:2] + [*y] + x[3:]
print(x)
x.sort( )
print(x)
```

Output

```
[1, 3, [2, 4, 6, 8], 7, 9]
[1, 3, 2, 4, 6, 8, 7, 9]
[1, 2, 3, 4, 6, 7, 8, 9]
```

(b) Suppose a list contains 20 integers generated randomly. Receive a number from the keyboard and report position of all occurrences of this number in the list.

Program

```
# Report number of occurrences of a number in the list
import random
lst = [ ]
for k in range(20) :
    n = random.randint(0, 50)
    lst.append(n)
print(lst)

num = int(input('Enter number: '))
for i in range(len(lst)) :
    if lst[i] == num:
        print('Number found at position:', i)
```

Output

```
[44, 4, 22, 11, 36, 29, 38, 32, 14, 34, 48, 49, 4, 14, 23, 5, 28, 43, 49,
3]
Enter number: 14
Number found at position: 8
Number found at position: 13
```

(c) Suppose a list has 20 numbers. Write a program that removes all duplicates from this list.

Program

```
# Remove duplicates in a list
lst = [1, 2, 3, 4, 5, 1, 2, 3, 4, 5, 10, 20, 68, 8, 40, 45, 1, 5, 53, 45, 17]
print('Original list: ', lst)
final_lst=[ ]
for num in lst :
    if num not in final_lst :
        final_lst.append(num)

lst = final_lst
print('List after removing duplicates:', lst)
```

Output

```
Original list:  [1, 2, 3, 4, 5, 1, 2, 3, 4, 5, 10, 20, 68, 8, 40, 45, 1, 5, 53, 45, 17]
List after removing duplicates: [1, 2, 3, 4, 5, 10, 20, 68, 8, 40, 45, 53, 17]
```

(d) Suppose a list contains positive and negative numbers. Write a program to create two lists—one containing positive numbers and another containing negative numbers.

Program

```
# Separate positive and negative numbers into two lists
lst1 = [1, -9, -6, -45, -78,-1, 2, 3, 4, 5]
lst2 = [ ]
lst3 = [ ]
count, ncount = 0, 0
for num in lst1 :
    if num >= 0 :
        lst2.append(num)
    else :
        lst3.append(num)

print('Original list:', lst1)
print('Positive numbers list:', lst2)
print('Negative numbers list:', lst3)
```

Output

```
Original list: [1, -9, -6, -45, -78, -1, 2, 3, 4, 5]
Positive numbers list: [1, 2, 3, 4, 5]
Negative numbers list: [-9, -6, -45, -78, -1]
```

(e) Suppose a list contains 5 strings. Write a program to convert all these strings to uppercase.

Program

```
# Converts strings in a list to uppercase
lst = ['abc', 'def', 'ghi', 'jkl', 'lmn']
for i, item in enumerate(lst) :
    lst[i] = item.upper( )

print(lst)
```

Output

```
['ABC', 'DEF', 'GHI', 'JKL', 'LMN']
```

(f) Write a program that converts a list of temperatures in Fahrenheit degrees to equivalent Celsius degrees.

Program

```
# Conver farhrenheit temperatures in list into centigrade
fahr = [212, 120, 100, 93, 37]
for i, f in enumerate(fahr) :
    c = int(5 / 9 * (f - 32))
    fahr[i] = c
    print(f, c)
print(fahr)
```

Output

```
212 100
120 48
100 37
93 33
37 2
[100, 48, 37, 33, 2]
```

(g) Write a program to obtain a median value of a list of numbers, without disturbing the order of the numbers in the list.

Program

```
# Obtain median of a list
num = [1, 2, 3, 4, 5, 6, 7]
n = len(num)
if n % 2 == 0 :
   i = int(n / 2 - 1)
   j = int(n / 2)
   median = (num[i] + num[j]) / 2
else :
   i = int(n / 2)
   median = num[i]

print('Median value =', median)
```

Output

```
Median value = 4
```

(h) A list contains only positive and negative integers. Write a program to obtain the number of negative numbers present in the list, without using a loop.

Program

```
# Count negatives in a list without using a loop
lst = [1, 2, 3, 4, 5, -1, -2, -3, -4, -5]
if 0 not in lst :
   lst.append(0)
lst = sorted(lst)
pos = lst.index(0)
print('Number of negative numbers in the list =', pos)
```

Output

```
Number of negative numbers in the list = 5
```

(i) Suppose a list contains several words. Write a program to create another list that contains the first character of each word present in the first list.

Program

```
msg = ['Dialogue', 'is', 'dead', 'Chatalogue', 'is', 'in']
abbrmsg = [ ]
for word in msg :
    abbrmsg.append(word[0])
print(abbrmsg)
```

Output

```
['D', 'i', 'd', 'C', 'i', 'i']
```

(j) A list contains 10 numbers. Write a program to eliminate all duplicates from the list.

Program

```
# Eliminate all duplicates from the list
lst1= [1, 2, 1, 3, 4, 5, 6, 5, 2, 4]
lst2 = [ ]
print('Original list =', lst1)
for i in lst1 :
    if i not in lst2 :
        lst2.append(i)
print('List after eliminating duplicates =', lst2)
```

Output

```
[1, 2, 3, 4, 5, 6]
```

(k) Write a program to find the mean, median and mode of a list of 10 numbers.

Program

```
# Find the Mean, Median, Mode in a list of 10 numbers
lst = [10, 20, 30, 40, 30, 60, 70, 30, 80, 30]

# Mean
n = len(lst)
```

```
lst_sum = sum(lst)
mean = lst_sum / n

# Median
n = len(lst)
lst.sort()
if n % 2 == 0 :
   median1 = lst[ n // 2]
   median2 = lst[n // 2 - 1]
   median = ( median1 + median2 ) / 2
else :
   median = lst[ n // 2 ]

# Mode
lst1 = [0, 0]
for num in lst :
   occ = lst.count(num)
   if occ > lst1[0] :
      lst1 = [occ, num]

print('List =', lst)
print('Mean =', mean)
print('Median =', median)
print('Mode =', lst1[1])
```

Output

```
List = [10, 20, 30, 30, 30, 30, 40, 60, 70, 80]
Mean = 40.0
Median = 30.0
Mode = 30
```

9 Tuples

Let Us Python Solutions

7th Edition

[A] Which of the following properties apply to string, list and tuple?

- Iterable
- Sliceable
- Indexable
- Immutable
- Sequence
- Can be empty
- Sorted collection
- Ordered collection
- Unordered collection
- Elements can be accessed using their position in the collection

Answer

Iterable - string, list and tuple
Sliceable - string, list and tuple
Indexable - string, list and tuple
Immutable - string, tuple
Sequence - string, list and tuple
Can be empty - string, list and tuple
Sorted collection - none
Ordered collection - string, list and tuple
Unordered collection - set
Elements can be accessed using their position in the collection - string, list and tuple

[B] Which of the following operations can be performed on string, list and tuple?

- a = b + c
- a += b
- Appending a new element at the end
- Deletion of an element at the 0th position
- Modification of the last element
- In place reversal

Answer

a = b + c - string, list and tuple
a += b - string, list and tuple
Appending a new element at the end - list
Deletion of an element at the 0th position - list

Modification of last element - string, list and tuple
In place reversal - list

[C] Answer the following:

(a) Is this a valid tuple?

```
tpl = ('Square')
```

Answer

No. Correct way to create the tuple would be

```
tpl = ('Square',)
```

(b) What will be the output of the following code snippet?

```
num1 = num2 = (10, 20, 30, 40, 50)
print(id(num1), type(num2))
print(isinstance(num1, tuple))
print(num1 is num2)
print(num1 is not num2)
print(20 in num1)
print(30 not in num2)
```

Program

```
40291816 <class 'tuple'>
True
True
False
True
False
```

(c) Suppose a date is represented as a tuple (d, m, y). Write a program to create two date tuples and find the number of days between the two dates.

Program

```
# Determine number of days between two dates
dt1 = (17, 3, 1998)
dt2 = (17, 4, 2011)

d1, m1, y1 = dt1[0], dt1[1], dt1[2]
```

```
d2, m2, y2 = dt2[0], dt2[1], dt2[2]
days1 = [31, 0, 31, 30, 31, 30, 31, 31, 30, 31, 30, 31]
days2 = [31, 0, 31, 30, 31, 30, 31, 31, 30, 31, 30, 31]

ndays1 = (y1 - 1) * 365
ldays1 = ((y1 - 1) // 4) - ((y1 - 1) // 100) + ((y1 - 1) // 400)
tdays1 = ndays1 + ldays1

if((y1 % 4 == 0 and y1 % 100 != 0) or (y1 % 400 == 0)) :
    days1[1] = 29
else :
    days1[1] = 28

s1 = sum(days1[0:m1 - 1])
tdays1 += s1

ndays2 = (y2 - 1) * 365
ldays2 = ((y2 -1) // 4) - ((y2 - 1) // 100) + ((y2 - 1) // 400)
tdays2 = ndays2 + ldays2

if((y2 % 4 == 0 and y2 % 100 != 0) or (y2 % 400 == 0)) :
    days2[1] = 29
else :
    days2[1] = 28

s2 = sum(days2[0:m2 - 1])
tdays2 += s2

diff = tdays2 - tdays1
print('Difference in days = ', diff)
```

Output

```
Difference in days =  4779
```

(d) Create a list of tuples. Each tuple should contain an item and its price in float. Write a program to sort the tuples in descending order by price. Hint: Use **operator.itemgetter( )**.

Program

```
import operator
```

```
lst = [('Key', 101.25), ('Lock', 320.85), ('Hammer', 100.55),
('Spanner', 67.77), ('Tong', 93.03)]
print(sorted(lst, reverse = True, key = operator.itemgetter(1)))
```

Output

```
[('Lock', 320.85), ('Key', 101.25), ('Hammer', 100.55), ('Tong', 93.03),
('Spanner', 67.77)]
```

(e) Store the data about shares held by a user as tuples containing the following information about shares:

Share name
Date of purchase
Cost price
Number of shares
Selling price

Write a program to determine:

- Total cost of the portfolio.
- Total amount gained or lost.
- Percentage profit made, or loss incurred.

Program

```
lst = [ ]
i = 0

num_companies = int(input('Enter no. of companies: '))
for i in range(num_companies):
    name = input('Enter name: ')
    no_of_shares = int(input('Enter no of shares: '))
    dt_of_pur = input('Enter date of purchase: ')
    cost_price = int(input('Enter Cost price: '))
    selling_price = int(input('Enter selling price: '))
    tpl = (name, no_of_shares, dt_of_pur, cost_price, selling_price)
    lst.append(tpl)

tot = 0
gaintot = 0
losstot = 0
for l in lst :
```

```
    no_of_shares = l[1]
    cost_price = l[3]
    selling_price = l[4]
    cop = int(no_of_shares * cost_price)
    tot = tot + cop

    if selling_price > cost_price :
        gaintot += (selling_price - cost_price) * no_of_shares
    else :
        losstot += (cost_price - selling_price) * no_of_shares

print(f'Total cost of portfolio:{tot:.2f}')

if gaintot > losstot :
    net = gaintot - losstot
    gain_per = net / tot * 100
    print(f'Net amount gained:{net:.2f}')
    print(f'Percentage profit:{gain_per:.2f}')
else :
    net = losstot - gaintot
    loss_per = net / tot * 100
    print(f'Net amount lost:{net:.2f}')
    print(f'Percentage loss:{loss_per:.2f}')
```

Output

```
Enter no. of companies: 3
Enter name: L and T
Enter no of shares: 100
Enter date of purchase: 12/12/2012
Enter Cost price: 145
Enter selling price: 186
Enter name: Tata Motors
Enter no of shares: 120
Enter date of purchase: 13/11/2016
Enter Cost price: 785
Enter selling price: 678
Enter name: Infosys
Enter no of shares: 90
Enter date of purchase: 14/05/2018
Enter Cost price: 775
Enter selling price: 800
```

Total cost of portfolio: 178450.00
Net amount lost: 6490.00
Percentage loss: 3.64

(f) Write a program to remove empty tuples from a list of tuples.

Program

```
lst1= [( ), ('Paras', 5), ('Ankit', 11), ( ), ('Harsha', 115), ('Aditya', 115),
( ), ('Aditi', 3), ( )]
lst2 = [ ]
for item in lst1 :
   if len(item) != 0 :
      lst2.append(item)
print(lst2)
```

Output

```
[('Paras', 5), ('Ankit', 11), ('Harsha', 115), ('Aditya', 115), ('Aditi', 3)]
```

(g) Write a program to create the following 3 lists:
- a list of names
- a list of roll numbers
- a list of marks

Generate and print a list of tuples containing name, roll number and marks from the 3 lists. From this list generate 3 tuples—one containing all names, another containing all roll numbers and third containing all marks.

Program

```
name = ['Aditi' , 'Mrunal' , 'Aditya' , 'Girish' , 'Ankit' , 'Meenal']
rollno = ['12' , '43' , '45' , '50' , '66' , '21']
marks = ['90' , '45' , '82' , '75' , '95' , '65']
t1 = tuple(name)
t2 = tuple(rollno)
t3 = tuple(marks)
lst = [t1, t2, t3]
print(lst)
print(t1)
print(t2)
print(t3)
```

Output

[('Aditi', 'Mrunal', 'Aditya', 'Girish', 'Ankit', 'Meenal'), ('12', '43', '45', '50', '66', '21'), ('90', '45', '82', '75', '95', '65')]
('Aditi', 'Mrunal', 'Aditya', 'Girish', 'Ankit', 'Meenal')
('12', '43', '45', '50', '66', '21')
('90', '45', '82', '75', '95', '65')

[D] Match the following for the values each **range( )** function will generated when used in a **for** loop.

a. tpl1 = ('A',)	1. tuple of length 6
b. tpl1 = ('A')	2. tuple of lists
c. t = tpl[::-1]	3. Tuple
d. ('A', 'B', 'C', 'D')	4. list of tuples
e. [(1, 2), (2, 3), (4, 5)]	5. String
f. tpl = tuple(range(2, 5))	6. Sorts tuple
g. ([1, 2], [3, 4], [5, 6])	7. (2, 3, 4)
h. t = tuple('Ajooba')	8. tuple of strings
i. [*a, *b, *c]	9. Unpacking of tuples in a list
j. (*a, *b, *c)	10. Unpacking of lists in a tuple

Answer

tpl1 = ('A',) - Tuple
tpl1 = ('A') - String
t = tpl[::-1] - Sorts tuple
('A' , 'B' , 'C' , 'D') - tuple of strings
[(1, 2), (2, 3), (4, 5)] - list of tuples
tpl = tuple(range(2, 5)) - (2, 3, 4)
([1, 2], [3, 4], [5, 6]) - tuple of lists
t = tuple('Ajooba') - tuple of length 6
[*a , *b, *c] - Unpacking of tuples in a list
(*a , *b, *c) - Unpacking of lists in a tuple

10 Sets

Let Us Python Solutions

7th Edition

[A] What will be the output of the following programs?

(a)
```
s = {1, 2, 3, 7, 6, 4}
s.discard(10)
s.remove(10)
print(s)
```

Output

Element 10 is not present in set **s. discard( )** would do nothing, whereas, **remove( )** would report an error.

(b)
```
s1 = {10, 20, 30, 40, 50}
s2 = {10, 20, 30, 40, 50}
print(id(s1), id(s2))
```

Output

40530296 40530184

(c)
```
s1 = {10, 20, 30, 40, 50}
s2 = {10, 20, 30, 40, 50}
s3 = {*s1, *s2}
print(s3)
```

Output

{40, 10, 50, 20, 30}

(d)
```
s = set('KanLabs')
t = s[::-1]
print(t)
```

Output

Error: set is not a subscriptable object. In other words [ ] cannot be used with a set.

(e)
```
num = {10, 20, {30, 40}, 50}
print(num)
```

Output

Error: Nested sets are illegal.

(f)
```
s = {'Tiger', 'Lion', 'Jackal'}
del(s)
print(s)
```

Output

Error: name 's' is not defined. This happens because **del( )** deletes the set object.

(g)
```
fruits = {'Kiwi', 'Jack Fruit', 'Lichi'}
fruits.clear( )
print(fruits)
```

Output

set( ). After calling **clear( )**, **fruits** becomes an empty set.

(h)
```
s = {10, 25, 4, 12, 3, 8}
s = sorted(s)
print(s)
```

Output

[3, 4, 8, 10, 12, 25]

(i)
```
s = { }
t = {1, 4, 5, 2, 3}
print(type(s), type(t))
```

Output

<class 'dict'> <class 'set'>

[B] Answer the following:

(a) A set contains names which begin either with A or with B. Write a program to separate out the names into two sets, one containing names beginning with A and another containing names beginning with B.

Program

```
# Split given set into two sets
```

```
lst = {'Aditya', 'Aditi', 'Ankita', 'Aniket', 'Anuja', 'Bhushan', 'Bahu',
'Bali', 'Bhoomi', 'Babhoti' }
t = set( )
s = set( )
for item in lst :
    if item.startswith('A') :
        t.add(item)
    elif item.startswith('B') :
        s.add(item)
print(s)
print(t)
```

Output

```
{'Bhoomi', 'Bahu', 'Babhoti', 'Bali', 'Bhushan'}
{'Anuja', 'Ankita', 'Aditya', 'Aniket', 'Aditi'}
```

(b) Create an empty set. Write a program that adds five new names to this set, modifies one existing name and deletes two names existing in it.

Program

```
# Set operations
s = set( )
s.add('Amol')
s.add('Priya')
s.add('Mira')
s.add('Dipti')
s.add('Anil')
print('After adding 5 names:', s)
s.remove('Anil')
s.add('ANIL')
print('After modifying Anil:', s)
s.remove('Dipti')
s.remove('Mira')
print('After deleting Dipti and Mira:', s)
```

Output

```
After adding 5 names: {'Priya', 'Dipti', 'Anil', 'Mira', 'Amol'}
After modifying Anil: {'Priya', 'ANIL', 'Dipti', 'Mira', 'Amol'}
After deleting Dipti and Mira: {'Priya', 'ANIL', 'Amol'}
```

(c) What is the difference between the two set functions—**discard( )** and **remove( )**.

Answer

remove( ) raises an exception when the element which we are trying to remove is not present in the set, whereas, **discard( )** doesn't.

(d) Write a program to create a set containing 10 randomly generated numbers in the range 15 to 45. Count how many of these numbers are less than 30. Delete all numbers which are greater than 35.

Program

```
# Set operations
import random
s = set( )
while True :
    s.add(random.randint(15, 45))
    if len(s) == 10 :
        break
print('Oringal set:', s)
t = set( )
count = 0
for item in s :
    if item < 30 :
        count += 1
    if item <= 35 :
        t.add(item)

s = t
print('Count of nos. less than 30:', count)
print('Set after deleting elements > 35: ', s)
```

Output

```
Oringal set: {32, 34, 40, 15, 16, 22, 23, 24, 25, 27}
Count of nos. less than 30: 7
Set after deleting elements > 35:  {32, 34, 15, 16, 22, 23, 24, 25, 27}
```

(e) What do the following set operators do?

|, &, ^, -

Answer

| Union of two sets
& Intersection of two sets
^ Symmetric difference between two sets
- Difference between two sets

(f) What do the following set operators do?

|=, &=, ^=, -=

Answer

|= performs union of two sets and stores the result in left operand.

&= performs intersection of two sets and stores result in left operand.

^= Finds symmetric difference between two sets and stores result in left operand.

-= Finds difference between two sets and stores result in left operand.

(g) How will you remove all duplicate elements present in a string, a list and a tuple?

Answer

```
# Delete duplicates from string, list and tuple
s = 'Razmattaz'
s = ''.join(sorted(set(s), key = s.index))
print(s)
lst = ['R', 'a', 'a', 'z', 'm', 'a', 't', 't', 'a', 'z']
lst = list(sorted(set(lst), key = lst.index))
print(lst)
tpl = ('R', 'a', 'a', 'z', 'm', 'a', 't', 't', 'a', 'z')
tpl = tuple(sorted(set(tpl), key = tpl.index))
print(tpl)
```

Output

```
Razmt
['R', 'a', 'z', 'm', 't']
```

```
('R', 'a', 'z', 'm', 't')
```

(h) Which operator is used for determining whether a set is a subset of another set?

Answer

The '<' operator is used to determine whether a set is a subset of another set. The corresponding method is **issubset( )**, which gives the same result.

```
s = {12, 15, 13, 23, 22, 16, 17}
t = {13, 15, 22}
print(t.issubset(s))        # print True
print(t < s)                # print True
```

(i) What will be the output of the following program?

```
s = {'Mango', 'Banana', 'Guava', 'Kiwi'}
s.clear( )
print(s)
del(s)
print(s)
```

Program

```
set( )
NameError: name 's' is not defined
```

(j) Which of the following is the correct way to create an empty set?

```
s1 = set( )
s2 = { }
```

What are the types of **s1** and **s2**? How will you confirm the type?

Answer

s1 = set( ) is the correct way to create an empty set.
s2 = { } is the correct way to create an empty dictionary.

Types of **s1** and **s2** can be confirmed as shown below:

```
s1 = set( )
s2 = { }
```

```
print(type(s1))
print(type(s2))
```

Its output will be:

```
<class 'set'>
<class 'dict'>
```

11 Dictionaries

Let Us Python Solutions

7th Edition

[A] State whether the following statements are True or False:

(a) Dictionary elements can be accessed using position-based index.

Answer

False

(b) Dictionaries are immutable.

Answer

False

(c) Insertion order is preserved by a dictionary.

Answer

False

(d) The very first key - value pair in a dictionary **d** can be accessed using the expression **d[0]**.

Answer

False

(e) **courses.clear( )** will delete the dictionary object called **courses**.

Answer

False

(f) It is possible to nest dictionaries.

Answer

True

(g) It is possible to hold multiple values against a key in a dictionary.

Answer

True

[B] Attempt the following questions:

(a) Write a program that reads a string from the keyboard and creates dictionary containing frequency of each character occurring in the string. Also print these occurrences in the form of a histogram.

Program

```
# Count frequency of characters in string
s = input('Enter any string: ')
freq = { }
for ch in s :
```

```
    if ch in freq :
        freq[ch] += 1
    else :
        freq[ch] = 1
print ('Count of all characters is: ', freq)

for k, v in freq.items( ) :
    print(k, ':', end = '')
    for i in range(0, v) :
        print('*', end ='')
    print( )
```

Output

```
Enter any string: Ashish Samant
Count of all characters is:  {'A': 1, 's': 2, 'h': 2, 'i': 1, ' ': 1, 'S': 1, 'a': 2, 'm': 1, 'n': 1, 't': 1}
A :*
s :**
h :**
i :*
  :*
S :*
a :**
m :*
n :*
t :*
```

(b) Create a dictionary containing names of students and marks obtained by them in three subjects. Write a program to replace the marks in three subjects with the total in three subjects, and average marks. Also report the topper of the class.

Program

```
# Dictionary operations
import operator
students = {
                'Dipti' : { 'Maths' : 48, 'eng' : 60, 'hindi' : 95},
                'Smriti' : { 'Maths' : 75,'eng' : 68,'hindi' : 89},
                'Subodh' : { 'Maths' : 45,'eng' : 66,'hindi' : 87}
        }
```

```
tot = { }
topper_name = ''
topper_marks = 0
for nam, info in students.items( ) :
    total = 0
    for sub, marks in info.items( ) :
        total = total + marks

    avg = int(total / 3)
    students[nam] = {'Total' : total, 'Average' : avg}
    if avg > topper_marks :
        topper_name = nam
        topper_marks = avg

print(students)
print ('Topper of the class:' , topper_name)
print('Topper marks:', topper_marks)
```

Output

```
{'Dipti': {'Total': 203, 'Average': 67}, 'Smriti': {'Total': 232, 'Average':
77}, 'Subodh': {'Total': 198, 'Average': 66}}
Topper of the class: Smriti
Topper marks: 77
```

(c) Given the following dictionary:

```
portfolio = { 'accounts' :  [ 'SBI' , 'IOB'],
              'shares' :  ['HDFC' , 'ICICI' , 'TM' , 'TCS'],
              'ornaments' : ['10 gm gold', '1 kg silver']}
```

Write a program to perform the following operations:

- Add a key to portfolio called 'MF' with values 'Reliance' and 'ABSL'.
- Set the value of 'accounts' to a list containing 'Axis' and 'BOB'.
- Sort the items in the list stored under the 'shares' key.
- Delete the list stored under 'ornaments' key.

Program

```
# Dictionary operations
portfolio = {
                'accounts' : [ 'SBI', 'IOB'],
```

```
                    'shares' : ['HDFC', 'ICICI', 'TM', 'TCS'],
                    'ornaments' : ['10 gm gold', '1 kg silver']
          }

portfolio['MF'] = ['Reliance','ABSL']
print(portfolio)

portfolio['accounts'] = ['Axis', 'BOB']
print(portfolio)

lst = portfolio['shares']
portfolio['shares'] = sorted(lst)
print(portfolio)

del(portfolio['ornaments'])
print(portfolio)
```

Output

```
{'accounts': ['SBI', 'IOB'], 'shares': ['HDFC', 'ICICI', 'TM', 'TCS'],
'ornaments': ['10 gm gold', '1 kg silver'], 'MF': ['Reliance', 'ABSL']}
{'accounts': ['Axis', 'BOB'], 'shares': ['HDFC', 'ICICI', 'TM', 'TCS'],
'ornaments': ['10 gm gold', '1 kg silver'], 'MF': ['Reliance', 'ABSL']}
{'accounts': ['Axis', 'BOB'], 'shares': ['HDFC', 'ICICI', 'TCS', 'TM'],
'ornaments': ['10 gm gold', '1 kg silver'], 'MF': ['Reliance', 'ABSL']}
{'accounts': ['Axis', 'BOB'], 'shares': ['HDFC', 'ICICI', 'TCS', 'TM'], 'MF':
['Reliance', 'ABSL']}
```

(d) Create two dictionaries—one containing grocery items and their prices and another containing grocery items and quantity purchased. By using the values from these two dictionaries compute the total bill.

Program

```
# Calculate total bill amount
prices = { 'Bottles' : 30, 'Tiffin' : 100, 'Bag' : 400, 'Bicycle' : 2000 }
stock = { 'Bottles' : 10 , 'Tiffin' : 8, 'Bag' : 1, 'Bicycle' : 5}
total = 0
for key in prices :
   value = prices[key] * stock[key]
   total += value
```

```
print('Total Bill Amount =' , total)
```

Output

```
Bottles 300
Tiffin 800
Bag 400
Bicycle 10000
Total Bill Amount = 11500
```

(e) Which functions will you use to fetch all keys, all values and key value pairs from a given dictionary?

Answer

To fetch all keys - **keys( )**
To fetch all values - **values( )**
To fetch key value pairs - **items( )**

(f) Create a dictionary of 10 usernames and passwords. Receive the username and password from keyboard and search for them in the dictionary. Print appropriate message on the screen based on whether a match is found or not.

Program

```
# Check authentic user
users = {
            'Sanjay' : 'ceftum1250', 'Rahul' : 'Crocin100',
            'Sanket' : 'Metrogyl50', 'Shyam' : 'Miopass10',
            'Satish' : 'mvpxx_9000', 'Srishti' : 'Relaxo!',
            'Smriti' : 'newyear200', 'Sakhi' : 'Bday1711',
            'Raakhi' : 'jallosh200', 'Rahika' : 'Ultu1900'
        }
userid = input('Enter username: ')
password = input('Enter password: ')

for k, v in users.items( ) :
    if k == userid and v == password :
        print('Valid username and password')
        exit( )

print('Invalid username and password')
```

Output

```
Enter username: Smriti
Enter password: newyear200
Valid username and password
```

(g) Given the following dictionary

```
marks = { 'Subu' : { 'Maths' : 88, 'Eng' : 60, 'SSt' : 95 },
          'Amol' : { 'Maths' : 78, 'Eng' : 68, 'SSt' : 89 },
          'Raka' : { 'Maths' : 56, 'Eng' : 66, 'SSt' : 77 }}
```

Write a program to perform the following operations:

- Print marks obtained by Amol in English.
- Set marks obtained by Raka in Maths to 77.
- Sort the dictionary by name.

Program

```
marks = {
            'Subu' : { 'Maths' : 88, 'Eng' : 60, 'SSt' : 95 },
            'Amol' : { 'Maths' : 78, 'Eng' : 68, 'SSt' : 89 },
            'Raka' : { 'Maths' : 56, 'Eng' : 66, 'SSt' : 77 }
        }
print('Marks obtained by Amol in english:', marks['Amol']['Eng'])
marks['Raka']['Maths'] = '77'
print(marks)
marks = dict(sorted(marks.items( )))
print(marks)
```

Output

```
Marks obtained by Amol in english: 68
{'Subu': {'Maths': 88, 'Eng': 60, 'SSt': 95}, 'Amol': {'Maths': 78, 'Eng':
68, 'SSt': 89}, 'Raka': {'Maths': 56, 'Eng': 66, 'SSt': 77}}
{'Amol': {'Maths': 78, 'Eng': 68, 'SSt': 89}, 'Raka': {'Maths': 56, 'Eng':
66, 'SSt': 77}, 'Subu': {'Maths': 88, 'Eng': 60, 'SSt': 95}}
```

(h) Create a dictionary which stores the following data:

Interface	**IP Address**	**status**
eth0	1.1.1.1	up
eth1	2.2.2.2	up
wlan0	3.3.3.3	down

```
wlan1      4.4.4.4         up
```

Write a program to perform the following operations:
- Find the status of the given interface.
- Find the interface and IP of all interfaces which are up.
- Find the total number of interfaces.
- Add two new entries to the dictionary.

Program

```
# Working with nested directories
ifs = {
            'eth0':{'IP' : '1.1.1.1', 'Status' : 'up'},
            'eth1':{'IP' : '2.2.2.2', 'Status' : 'up'},
            'wlan0':{'IP' : '3.3.3.3', 'Status' : 'down'},
            'wlan1':{'IP' : '4.4.4.4', 'Status' : 'up'}
      }
test = input('Enter interface: ')
print(ifs[test]['Status'])

for k, v in ifs.items( ) :
   if v['Status'] == 'up' :
      print(k, v['IP'])

print('Total interfaces = ', len(ifs))

ifs['eth2'] = {'IP' : '5.5.5.5', 'Status' :'down'}
ifs['wlan2'] = {'IP' : '6.6.6.6', 'Status' : 'up'}
for k, v in ifs.items( ) :
   print(k, v)
```

Output

```
Enter interface: eth1
up
eth0 1.1.1.1
eth1 2.2.2.2
wlan1 4.4.4.4
Total interfaces = 4
eth0 {'IP': '1.1.1.1', 'Status': 'up'}
eth1 {'IP': '2.2.2.2', 'Status': 'up'}
wlan0 {'IP': '3.3.3.3', 'Status': 'down'}
```

```
wlan1 {'IP': '4.4.4.4', 'Status': 'up'}
eth2 {'IP': '5.5.5.5', 'Status': 'down'}
wlan2 {'IP': '6.6.6.6', 'Status': 'up'}
```

(i) Suppose a dictionary contains 5 key-value pairs of name and marks. Write a program to print them from last pair to first pair. Keep deleting every pair printed, such that the end of printing the dictionary falls empty.

Program

```
marks = { 'Subu' : 88, 'Amol' : 78, 'Raka' : 56, 'Dinesh' : 68, 'Ranjit' :
88}
l = len(marks)
for i in range(l) :
    print(marks.popitem( ))
print(marks)
```

[C] Answer the following questions:

(a) What will be the output of the following code snippet?

```
d = { 'Milk' : 1, 'Soap' : 2, 'Towel' : 3, 'Shampoo' : 4, 'Milk' : 7}
print(d[0], d[1], d[2])
```

Answer

Error: Dictionary elements cannot be accessed using a position-based index.

(b) Which of the following statements are CORRECT?

i. A dictionary will always contain unique keys.
ii. Each key in a dictionary may have multiple values.
iii. If same key is assigned a different value, latest value will prevail.

Answer

i. True
ii. True
iii. True

(c) How will you create an empty list, empty tuple, empty set and empty dictionary?

Answer

```
l = [ ]
t = ( )
s = set( )
d = { }
```

(d) How will you create a list, tuple, set and dictionary, each containing one element?

Program

```
l = [10]
t = (10,)
s = {10}
d = {10: 'A'}
```

(e) Given the following dictionary:

```
d = { 'd1': {'Fruitname' : 'Mango', 'Season' : 'Summer'},
      'd2': {'Fruitname' : 'Orange', 'Season' : 'Winter'}}
```

How will you access and print Mango and Winter?

Program

```
d = { 'd1': {'Fruitname' : 'Mango', 'Season' : 'Summer'},
      'd2': {'Fruitname' : 'Orange', 'Season' : 'Winter'}}
print(d['d1']['Fruitname'])
print(d['d2']['Season'])
```

(f) In the following table check the box if a property is enjoyed by the data types mentioned in columns?

Property	str	list	tuple	set	dict
Object	✓	✓	✓	✓	✓
Collection	✓	✓	✓	✓	✓
Mutable		✓		✓	✓
Ordered	✓	✓	✓		
Indexed by position	✓	✓	✓		
Indexed by key					✓
Iterable	✓	✓	✓	✓	✓
Slicing allowed	✓	✓	✓		

Nesting allowed	✓	✓	✓		✓
Homogeneous elements	✓			✓	✓
Heterogeneous elements		✓	✓		

(g) What is the most common usage of the data types mentioned below?
str
list
tuple
set
dict

Answer

str - collection of characters
list - similar elements
tuple - pairs or triplets
set - unique elements
dict - key-value pairs

12

Comprehensions

Let Us Python Solutions 7th Edition

[A] State whether the following statements are True or False:

(a) Tuple comprehension offers a fast and compact way to generate a tuple.

Answer

True

(b) List comprehension and dictionary comprehension can be nested.

Answer

True

(c) A list being used in a list comprehension cannot be modified when it is being iterated.

Answer

True

(d) Sets being immutable cannot be used in comprehension.

Answer

False

(e) Comprehension can be used to create a list, set or a dictionary.

Answer

True

[B] Answer the following questions:

(a) Write a program that generates a list of integer coordinates for all points in the first quadrant from (1, 1) to (5, 5). Use list comprehension.

Program

```
coord = [(x, y) for x in range(1, 6)for y in range(1, 6)]
print(coord)
```

Output

```
[(1, 1), (1, 2), (1, 3), (1, 4), (1, 5), (2, 1), (2, 2), (2, 3), (2, 4), (2, 5), (3,
1), (3, 2), (3, 3), (3, 4), (3, 5), (4, 1), (4, 2), (4, 3), (4, 4), (4, 5), (5, 1),
(5, 2), (5, 3), (5, 4), (5, 5)]
```

(b) Using list comprehension, write a program to create a list by multiplying each element in the list by 10.

Program

```
lst = [-7, 10, 34, 2, 5, 45, 67]
lst = [(x * 10) for x in lst]
print(lst))
```

Output

```
[-70, 100, 340, 20, 50, 450, 670]
```

(c) Write a program to generate first 20 Fibonacci numbers using list comprehension.

Program

```
lst = [0, 1]
[lst.append(lst[k - 1] + lst[k - 2]) for k in range(2, 20)]
print('First 20 Fibonacci numbers:', lst)
```

Output

```
First 20 Fibonacci numbers:
[0, 1, 1, 2, 3, 5, 8, 13, 21, 34, 55, 89, 144, 233, 377, 610, 987, 1597,
2584, 4181]
```

(d) Write a program to generate two lists using list comprehension. One list should contain first 20 odd numbers, and another should contain first 20 even numbers.

Program

```
lst1 = [x for x in range(40) if x % 2 != 0]
print('First 20 Odd Numbers:')
print(lst1)
lst2 = [x for x in range(40) if x % 2 == 0]
```

```
print('First 20 Even Numbers:')
print(lst2)
```

Output

```
First 20 Odd Numbers:
[1, 3, 5, 7, 9, 11, 13, 15, 17, 19, 21, 23, 25, 27, 29, 31, 33, 35, 37, 39]
First 20 Even Numbers:
[0, 2, 4, 6, 8, 10, 12, 14, 16, 18, 20, 22, 24, 26, 28, 30, 32, 34, 36, 38]
```

(e) Suppose a list contains positive and negative numbers. Write a program to create two lists—one containing positive numbers and another containing negative numbers.

Program

```
lst = [1, 2, 5, -11, -9, 10, 13, 15, -17, -19, -21, -23, 25, 27, -29]
pos = [num for num in lst if num > 0]
print(pos)
neg = [num for num in lst if num < 0]
print(neg)
```

Output

```
[1, 2, 5, 10, 13, 15, 25, 27]
[-11, -9, -17, -19, -21, -23, -29]
```

(f) Suppose a list contains 5 strings. Write a program to convert all these strings to uppercase.

Program

```
lst = ['abc', 'def', 'ghi', 'jkl', 'lmn']
lst = [s.upper( ) for s in lst]
print(lst)
```

Output

```
['ABC', 'DEF', 'GHI', 'JKL', 'LMN']
```

(g) Write a program that converts a list of temperatures in Fahrenheit degrees to equivalent Celsius degrees using list comprehension.

Program

```
farh = [101, 120, 100, 67, 32]
celsius = [(e - 32) * 5 / 9 for e in farh]
print(celsius)
```

Output

```
[38, 48, 37, 19, 0]
```

(h) Write a program to generate a 2D matrix of size 4 x 5 containing random multiples of 4 in the range 40 to 160.

Program

```
import random
rows, cols = (5, 4)
arr = [[(4 * random.randint(10, 40)) for i in range(cols)] for j in
range(rows)]
print(arr)
```

Output

```
[[72, 108, 92, 148], [88, 152, 76, 96], [148, 108, 104, 136], [132, 48,
160, 116], [140, 40, 104, 48]]
```

(i) Write a program that converts words present in a list into uppercase and stores them in a set.

Program

```
lst = ['function', 'office', 'type', 'product', 'most']
s = set([word.upper( ) for word in lst])
print(s)
```

Output

```
{'MOST', 'TYPE', 'FUNCTION', 'OFFICE', 'PRODUCT'}
```

[C] Attempt the following questions:

(a) Consider the following code snippet:

```
s = set([int(n) for n in input('Enter values: ').split( )])
print(s)
```

What will be the output of the above code snippet if input provided to it is 1 2 3 4 5 6 7 2 4 5 0?

Output

{0, 1, 2, 3, 4, 5, 6, 7}

(b) How will you convert the following code into a list comprehension?

```
a = [ ]
for n in range(10, 30) :
   if n % 2 == 0 :
      a.append(n)
```

Answer

```
a = [n for n in range(10, 30) if n % 2 == 0]
```

(c) How will you convert the following code into a set comprehension?

```
a = set( )
for n in range(21, 40) :
   if n % 2 == 0 :
      a.add(n)
print(a)
```

Answer

```
a = {n for n in range(21, 40) if n % 2 == 0}
```

(d) What will be the output of the following code snippet?

```
s = [a + b for a in ['They ', 'We '] for b in ['are gone!', 'have come!']]
print(s)
```

Answer

['They are gone!', 'They have come!', 'We are gone!', 'We have come!']

(e) From the sentence

```
sent = 'Pack my box with five dozen liquor jugs'
```

how will you generate a set given below?

{'liquor', 'jugs', 'with', 'five', 'dozen', 'Pack'}

Output

```
sent = 'Pack my box with five dozen liquor jugs'
sent = {w for w in sent.split( ) if len(w) > 3}
```

(f) Which of the following is the correct form of dictionary comprehension?

i. dict_var = {key : value for (key, value) in dictonary.items( )}
ii. dict_var = {key : value for (key, value) in dictonary}
iii. dict_var = {key : value for (key, value) in dictonary.keys( )}

Output

```
dict_var = {key : value for (key, value) in dictonary.items( )}
```

(g) Using comprehension how will you convert

{'a' : 1, 'b' : 2, 'c' : 3, 'd' : 4, 'e' : 5}

into

{'A' : 100, 'B' : 200, 'C' : 300, 'D' : 400, 'E' : 500}?

Output

```
d = {'a' : 1, 'b' : 2, 'c' : 3, 'd' : 4, 'e' : 5}
d = {key.upper( ) : value * 100 for (key, value) in d.items( )}
print(d)
```

(h) What will be the output of the following code snippet?

```
lst = [2, 7, 8, 6, 5, 5, 4, 4, 8]
s = {True if n % 2 == 0 else False for n in lst}
print(s)
```

Output

```
{False, True}
```

(i) How will you convert

d = {'AMOL' : 20, 'ANIL' : 12, 'SUNIL' : 13, 'RAMESH' : 10}

into

{'Amol': 400, 'Anil': 144, 'Sunil': 169, 'Ramesh': 100}

Output

```
d = {'AMOL' : 20, 'ANIL' : 12, 'SUNIL' : 13, 'RAMESH' : 10}
d = {key.capitalize( ) : value * value for (key, value) in d.items( )}
print(d)
```

(j) How will you convert the words present in a list given below into uppercase and store them in a set?

```
lst = ['Amol', 'Vijay', 'Vinay', 'Rahul', 'Sandeep']
```

Output

```
lst = ['Amol', 'Vijay', 'Vinay', 'Rahul', 'Sandeep']
d = {word.upper( ) for word in lst}
print(d)
```

13 Functions

[A] Answer the following questions:

(a) Write a program that defines a function **count_lower_upper( )** that accepts a string and calculates the number of uppercase and lowercase alphabets in it. It should return these values as a dictionary. Call this function for some sample strings.

Program

```
def count_lower_upper(s) :
    dlu = {'Lower' : 0, 'Upper' :  0}
    for ch in s :
        if ch.islower( ) :
            dlu['Lower'] += 1
        elif ch.isupper( ) :
            dlu['Upper'] += 1
    return(dlu)

d = count_lower_upper('James BOnd ')
print(d)
d = count_lower_upper('Anant Amrut Mahalle')
print(d)
```

Output

```
{'Lower': 6, 'Upper': 3}
{'Lower': 14, 'Upper': 3}
```

(b) Write a program that defines a function **compute( )** that calculates the value of n + nn + nnn + nnnn, where n is digit received by the function. Test the function for digits 4 and 7.

Program

```
import math
def compute(n) :
    s = 0
    num = 0
    for outer in range(0, 4) :
        num = num * 10 + n
        s = s + num
    return(s)
```

```
total = compute(7)
print('The value of n + nn + nnn + nnnn is', total)
total = compute(4)
print('The value of n + nn + nnn + nnnn is', total)
```

Output

```
The value of n + nn + nnn + nnnn is 8638
The value of n + nn + nnn + nnnn is 4936
```

(c) Write a program that defines a function **create_array( )** to create and return a 3D array whose dimensions are passed to the function. Also initialize each element of this array to a value passed to the function.

Program

```
def create_array(i, j, k, num):
  l = [[[num for col in range(k)] for row in range(j)] for twods in
range(i)]
  return(l)

lst = create_array(4, 3, 2, 10)
print(lst)
```

Output

```
[[[10, 10], [10, 10], [10, 10]], [[10, 10], [10, 10], [10, 10]], [[10, 10],
[10, 10], [10, 10]], [[10, 10], [10, 10], [10, 10]]]
```

(d) Write a program that defines a function **create_list( )** to create and return a list which is an intersection of two lists passed to it.

Program

```
def create_list(l1, l2) :
    l3 = list(set(l1) & set(l2))
    return(l3)

lst1 = [10, 20, 30, 40, 50]
lst2 = [1 ,2, 3, 40, 10]
lst3 = create_list(lst1, lst2)
print(lst3)
```

Output

[40, 10]

(e) Write a program that defines a function **sanitize_list( )** to remove all duplicate entries from the list that it receives.

Program

```
def sanitize_list(l) :
    l = list(set(l))
    return(l)

lst = [10, 3, 30, 10, 4, 3, -5, 10, 0, -5]
lst = sanitize_list(lst)
print('List after removing duplicates: ', lst)
```

Output

List after removing duplicates: [0, 3, 4, 10, -5, 30]

(f) Which of the calls to **print_it( )** in the following program will report errors?

```
def print_it(i, a, s, *args) :
        print( )
        print(i, a, s, end = ' ')
        for var in args :
                print(var, end = ' ')

print_it(10, 3.14)
print_it(20, s = 'Hi', a = 6.28)
print_it(a = 6.28, s = 'Hello', i = 30)
print_it(40, 2.35, 'Nag', 'Mum', 10)
```

Answer

The first call

print_it(10, 3.14)

will report an error 'missing 1 required positional argument: 's''

The other 3 calls are correct.

(g) Which of the calls to **fun( )** in the following program will report errors?

```
def fun(a, *args, s = '!') :
    print(a, s)
    for i in args :
            print(i, s)

fun(10)
fun(10, 20)
fun(10, 20, 30)
fun(10, 20, 30, 40, s = '+')
```

Answer

No error. All calls are correct.

[B] Attempt the following questions:

(a) What is being passed to function **fun( )** in the following code?

```
int a = 20
lst = [10, 20, 30, 40, 50]
fun(a, lst)
```

Answer

Address of int and address of list.

(b) Which of the following are valid **return** statements?

```
return (a, b, c)
return a + b + c
return a, b, c
```

Answer

All are valid return statements.

(c) What will be the output of the following program?

```
def fun( ) :
    print('First avatar')
fun( )
```

```
def fun( ) :
    print('New avatar')
fun( )
```

Answer

First avatar
New avatar

(d) How will you define a function containing three **return** statements, each returning a different type of value?

Answer

```
def fun(a) :
    if a < 0 :
        return 10
    if a == 0 :
        return 10.0
    if a > 0 :
        return '10'

print(fun(-5))
print(fun(5))
print(fun(0))
```

(e) Can function definitions be nested? If yes, why would you want to do so?

Answer

Function definitions can be nested. At times we need a function that is needed by only one function. This function can then be nested within the function that needs to call it.

(f) How will you call **print_it( )** to print elements of **tpl**?

```
def print_it(a, b, c, d, e) :
    print(a, b, c, d, e)
tpl = ('A', 'B', 'C', 'D', 'E')
```

Answer

```
print_it(*tpl)
```

14 Recursion

Let Us Python Solutions

7th Edition

[A] State whether the following statements are True or False:

(a) A recursive function is the one that calls another execution instance of the same function.

Answer

True

(b) If a recursive function uses three variables **a**, **b** and **c**, then the same set of variables are used during each recursive call.

Answer

False

(c) Multiple copies of the recursive function are created in memory.

Answer

False

(d) A recursive function must contain at least 1 **return** statement.

Answer

True

(e) Every iteration done using a **while** or **for** loop can be replaced with recursion.

Answer

True

(f) Logics expressible in the form of themselves are good candidates for writing recursive functions.

Answer

True

(g) Tail recursion is similar to a loop.

Answer

True

(h) Infinite recursion can occur if the base case is not properly defined.

Answer

True

(i) A recursive function is easy to write, understand and maintain as compared to a one that uses a loop.

Answer

False

[B] Answer the following questions :

(a) Write a program that calculates the sum of first 5 natural numbers using tail recursion. Rewrite the function to obtain the sum using head recursion.

```
def headsum(n) :
    if n != 0 :
        s = n + headsum(n - 1)
    else :
        return 0
    return s

print('Sum of First 5 Natural numbers = ', headsum(5))
```

Program

```
def headsum(n) :
    if n != 0 :
        s = n + headsum(n - 1)
    else :
        return 0
    return s

print('Sum of First 5 Natural numbers = ', headsum(5))
```

Output

```
Sum of First 5 Natural numbers = 15
```

(b) There are three pegs labeled A, B and C. Four disks are placed on peg A. The bottom-most disk is largest, and disks go on decreasing in size with the topmost disk being smallest. The objective of the game is to move the disks from peg A to peg C, using peg B as an auxiliary peg. The rules of the game are as follows:

- Only one disk may be moved at a time, and it must be the top disk on one of the pegs.
- A larger disk should never be placed on the top of a smaller disk.

Write a program to print out the sequence in which the disks should be moved such that all disks on peg A are finally transferred to peg C.

Program

```
def move(n, sp, ap, ep) :
    if n == 1 :
        print('Move from', sp ,'to', ep)
    else :
        move(n-1, sp, ep, ap)
        move(1, sp, '', ep)
        move(n-1, ap, sp, ep)

move(4, 'A', 'B', 'C')
```

Output

```
Move from A to B
Move from A to C
Move from B to C
Move from A to B
Move from C to A
Move from C to B
Move from A to B
Move from A to C
Move from B to C
Move from B to A
Move from C to A
Move from B to C
Move from A to B
Move from A to C
Move from B to C
```

(c) A string is entered through the keyboard. Write a recursive function that counts the number of vowels in this string.

Program

```
def fun(s, idx, count) :
    if idx == len(s):
        return count
    if s[idx] == 'a' or s[idx] == 'e' or s[idx] == 'i' or s[idx] == 'o'
            or s[idx] == 'u' :
        count += 1
    count = fun(s, idx + 1, count)
    return count

count = fun('Raindrops on roses', 0, 0)
print(count)
```

Output

```
6
```

(d) A string is entered through the keyboard. Write a recursive function removes any tabs present in this string.

Program

```
def replace(source, i, n) :
    global target
    if i == n :
        return
    if source[ i ] == '\t' :
        pass
    else :
        target += source[ i ]

    i += 1
    replace(source, i, n)

s = 'Raindrops	on	Roses and whiskers	on	kittens'
print(s)
target = ''
replace(s, 0, len(s) - 1)
print(target)
```

Output

```
Raindrops on       Roses and whiskers      on       kittens
RaindropsonRoses and whiskersonkitten
```

(e) A string is entered through the keyboard. Write a recursive function that checks whether the string is a palindrome or not.

Program

```
def ispalindrome(st, start, end) :
    if start > end :
        return True

    if st[start] != st[end] :
        return False

    status = ispalindrome(st, start + 1, end - 1)
    return status

st1 = 'malayalam'
st2 = 'malhindilam'
status = ispalindrome(st1, 0, len(st1) - 1)
print(status)
status = ispalindrome(st2, 0, len(st2) - 1)
print(status)
```

Output

```
True
False
```

(f) Two numbers are received through the keyboard into variables **a** and **b**. Write a recursive function that calculates the value of a^b.

Program

```
def power(x, y) :
    if y == 0 :
        return 1
    if y == 1 :
        return x
```

```
        prod = x * power(x, y - 1)
        return prod

c = power(2, 5)
print(c)
d = power(3, 4)
print(d)
```

Output

```
32
81
```

(g) Write a recursive function that reverses the list of numbers that it receives.

Program

```
def reverselist(lst, start, end) :
    if start > end :
        return

    lst[start], lst[end] = lst[end], lst[start]
    reverselist(lst, start + 1, end - 1)

numlst = [10, 20, 30, 40, 50]
reverselist(numlst, 0, 4)
print(numlst)
```

Output

```
[50, 40, 30, 20, 10]
```

(h) A list contains some negative and some positive numbers. Write a recursive function that sanitizes the list by replacing all negative numbers with 0.

Program

```
def replace(lst, i, n) :
    if i > n :
        return
    if lst[ i ] < 0 :
```

```
        lst[ i ] = 0

    i += 1
    replace( lst, i, n)

numlst = [10, 20, -3, -4, 50, -4, 60, 70, -4]
replace(numlst, 0, len(numlst) - 1)
print(numlst)
```

Output

```
[10, 20, 0, 0, 50, 0, 60, 70, 0]
```

(i) Write a recursive function to obtain average of all numbers present in a given list.

Program

```
def get_average(lst, n) :
    if n == 1 :
        return lst[ 0 ]
    else :
        return (get_average(lst, n - 1) * (n - 1) + lst[n - 1]) / n
    print(sum, n)
    return sum

numlst = [10, 20, 30, 40, 50, 60]
avg = get_average(numlst, len(numlst))
print(avg)
```

Output

```
35.0
```

(j) Write a recursive function to obtain length of a given string.

Program

```
def get_length(st) :
    if st == '' :
        return 0
    else :
        return 1 + get_length(st[1:])
```

```
s = 'www.ykanetkar.com'
l = get_length(s)
print(l)
```

Output

```
17
```

(k) Write a recursive function that receives a number as input and returns the square of the number. Use the mathematical identity $(n - 1)^2 = n^2 - 2n + 1$.

Program

```
def square(n) :
    if n < 0 :
        n = n * -1
    if n == 1 :
        return 1
    sq = square(n - 1) + 2 * n - 1
    return sq

s = square(4)
print(s)
s = square(-4)
print(s)
```

Output

```
16
16
```

[C] What will be the output of the following programs?

(a)
```
def fun(x, y) :
    if x == 0 :
        return y
    else :
        return fun(x - 1, x * y)
print(fun(4, 2))
```

Output

```
48
```

(b)
```
def fun(num) :
    if num > 100 :
        return num - 10
    return fun(fun(num + 11))
print(fun(75))
```

Output

```
91
```

(c)
```
def fun(num) :
    if num == 0 :
        print("False")
    if num == 1 :
        print("True")
    if num % 2 == 0 :
        fun(num / 2)
fun(256)
```

Output

```
True
```

15 Functional Programming

Let Us Python Solutions

7th Edition

[A] State whether the following statements are True or False:

(a) lambda function cannot be used with **reduce( )** function.

Answer

False

(b) lambda, **map( )**, **filter( )**, **reduce( )** can be combined in one single expression.

Answer

True

(c) Though functions can be assigned to variables, they cannot be called using these variables.

Program

False

(d) Functions can be passed as arguments to function and returned from function.

Program

True

(e) Functions can be built at execution time, the way lists, tuples, etc. can be.

Program

True

(f) Lambda functions are always nameless.

Program

True

[B] Using lambda, **map( )**, **filter( )** and **reduce( ) or a combination thereof to perform** the following tasks:

(a) Suppose a dictionary contains type of pet (cat, dog, etc.), name of pet and age of pet. Write a program that obtains the sum of all dog's ages.

Program

```
def fun1(d) :
    if d['Type'] == 'Dog' :
        return d['Age']
    else :
        return 0

def fun2(n) :
    if n == 0 :
        return False
    else :
        return True

dct = {
            'A101' : {'Type' : 'Cat', 'Name' : 'Tauby', 'Age' : 6 },
            'A102' : {'Type' : 'Dog', 'Name' : 'Tommy', 'Age' : 8 },
            'A103' : {'Type' : 'Dog', 'Name' : 'Tiger', 'Age' : 10 }
      }
lst2 = list(filter(fun2, list(map(fun1, list(dct.values( ))))))
print('The Sum of all Dogs ages:', sum(lst2)/len(lst2))
```

Output

```
The Sum of all Dogs ages: 9.0
```

(b) Consider the following list:

lst = [1.25, 3.22, 4.68, 10.95, 32.55, 12.54]

The numbers in the list represent radii of circles. Write a program to obtain a list of areas of these circles rounded off to two decimal places.

Program

```
lst = [1.25, 3.22, 4.68, 10.98, 32.55, 12.54]
area_lst = list(map(lambda n : round(n * n * 3.14, 2), lst))
print(area_lst)
```

Output

```
[4.91, 32.56, 68.77, 378.56, 3326.84, 493.77]
```

(c) Consider the following lists:

nums = [10, 20, 30, 40, 50, 60, 70, 80]
strs = ['A', 'B', 'C', 'D', 'E', 'F', 'G', 'H']

Write a program to obtain a list of tuples, where each tuple contains a number from one list and a string from another, in the same order in which they appear in the original lists.

Program

```
nums = [10, 20, 30, 40, 50, 60, 70, 80]
strs = ['A', 'B', 'C', 'D', 'E', 'F', 'G', 'H']
ltpl = list(map(lambda x, y : (x, y), nums, strs))
print(ltpl)
```

Output

```
[(10, 'A'), (20, 'B'), (30, 'C'), (40, 'D'), (50, 'E'), (60, 'F'), (70, 'G'), (80,
'H')]
```

(d) Suppose a dictionary contains names of students and marks obtained by them in an examination. Write a program to obtain a list of students who obtained more than 40 marks in the examination.

Program

```
students = {
                'Dipti' : 55, 'Smriti' :12, 'Subodh' :  45,
                'Meenal' : 33, 'Harsha' : 40 , 'Bhushan' : 42
          }
lst = filter(lambda x : x[1] >= 40, students.items( ))
print(list(lst))
```

Output

```
[('Dipti', 55), ('Subodh', 45), ('Harsha', 40), ('Bhushan', 42)]
```

(e) Consider the following list:

lst = ['Malayalam', 'Drawing', 'madamlamadam', '1234321']

Write a program to print out those strings which are palindromes.

Program

```
lst = ['Malayalam', 'Drawing', 'madamlamadam', '1234321']
lst1 = list(filter(lambda x : (x == ''.join(reversed(x))), lst))
print(lst1)
```

Output

```
['1234321']
```

(f) A list contains names of employees. Write a program to filter out those names whose length is more than 8 characters.

Program

```
lst = ['Parmeshwar', 'Kashmira', 'Seema', 'Roopa', 'Mahalaxmi']
lst1 = filter(lambda x : len(x) >= 8, lst)
print(list(lst1))
```

Output

```
['Parmeshwar', 'Kashmira', 'Mahalaxmi']
```

(g) A dictionary contains the following information about 5 employees:

First name
Last name
Age
Grade (Skilled, Semi-skilled, Highly-skilled)

Write a program to obtain a list of employees (first name + last name) who are Highly-skilled.

Program

```
d = {
        'Dinesh' : {'last_name' : 'Sahare', 'age' : 30, 'Grade' : 'Skilled'},
        'Ram' : {'last_name' : 'Jog', 'age' : 35, 'Grade' : 'Semi-Skilled'},
        'S.' : {'last_name' : 'Sam', 'age' : 25, 'Grade' : 'Highly-Skilled'},
        'Adi' : {'last_name' : 'Lim', 'age' : 25, 'Grade' : 'Highly-Skilled'},
        'Ann' : {'last_name' : 'Mir', 'age' : 25, 'Grade' : 'Highly-Skilled'}
    }
lst = filter(lambda x : x[1]['Grade'] == 'Highly-Skilled', d.items( ))
print(list(lst))
```

Output

```
[('S.', {'last_name': 'Sam', 'age': 25, 'Grade': 'Highly-Skilled'}), ('Adi', {'last_name': 'Lim', 'age': 25, 'Grade': 'Highly-Skilled'}), ('Ann', {'last_name': 'Mir', 'age': 25, 'Grade': 'Highly-Skilled'})]
```

(h) Consider the following list:

lst = ['Benevolent', 'Dictator', 'For', 'Life']

Write a program to obtain a string 'Benevolent Dictator For Life'.

Program

```
lst = ['Benevolent', 'Dictator', 'For', 'Life']
s = ' '.join(map(str, lst))
print(s)
```

Output

```
Benevolent Dictator For Life
```

(i) Consider the following list of students in a class.

lst = ['Rahul', 'Priya', 'Chaya', 'Narendra', 'Prashant']

Write a program to obtain a list in which all the names are converted to uppercase.

Program

```
lst = ['Rahul', 'Priya', 'Chaaya', 'Narendra', 'Prashant']
lst1 = map(lambda x : x.upper( ), lst)
print(list(lst1))
```

Output

```
['RAHUL', 'PRIYA', 'CHAYA', 'NARENDRA', 'PRASHANT']
```

16 Modules and Packages

Let Us Python Solutions

7th Edition

[A] Answer the following questions:

(a) Suppose there are three modules **m1.py, m2.py, m3.py**, containing functions **f1( ), f2( )** and **f3( )** respectively. How will you use those functions in your program?

Program

Directory structure will be as follows:

```
module
    __init__.py
    m1.py
    m2.py
    m3.py
client.py
```

The functions can be used as shown below:

```
# client.py
import module.m1
import module.m2
import module.m3

module.m1.f1( )
module.m2.f2( )
module.m3.f3( )
```

(b) Write a program containing functions **fun1( ), fun2( ), fun3( )** and some statements. Add suitable code to the program such that you can use it as a module or a normal program.

Program

```
def fun1( ) :
    print('Inside function fun1')

def fun2( ) :
    print('Inside function fun2')

def fun3( ) :
    print('Inside function fun3')

def main( ) :
```

```
    fun1( )
    fun2( )
    fun3( )

if (__name__ == '__main__') :
    main( )
```

(c) Suppose a module **mod.py** contains functions **f1( )**, **f2( )** and **f3( )**. Write 4 forms of import statements to use these functions in your program.

Program

```
Directory structure will be as follows:
module
    __init__.py
    mod.py
client.py

# client.py - Method 1
import module.mod
module.mod.f1( )
module.mod.f2( )
module.mod.f3( )

# client.py - Method 2
from module.mod import f1
from module.mod import f2
from module.mod import f3
f1( )
f2( )
f3( )

# client.py - Method 3
from module.mod import *
f1( )
f2( )
f3( )

# client.py - Method 4
import module.mod as M
```

```
M.f1( )
M.f2( )
M.f3( )
```

[B] Attempt the following questions:

(a) What is the difference between a module and a package?

Answer

A module is a .py file containing function definitions and statements. So, all .py files are modules.
A directory is treated as a package if it contains a file named __init__.py file in it.

(b) What is the purpose behind creating multiple packages and modules?

Answer

Multiple packages and modules are created to manage the complexity of code and to organize the code in reusable pieces.

(c) By default, to which module do the statements in a program belong? How do we access the name of this module?

Answer

By default, the statements in a program belong to __main__ module. We access the name of this module through the variable __name__.

(d) In the following statement what do **a**, **b**, **c**, **x** represent?

```
import a.b.c.x
```

Answer

a, b, c, x are nested modules.

(e) If module **m** contains a function **fun( )**, what is wrong with the following statements?

```
import m
fun( )
```

Answer

To call fun( ), we must use the syntax

m.fun( )

(f) What are the contents of **PYTHONPATH** variable? How can we access its contents programmatically?

Answer

PYTHONPATH environment variable contains a list of directories. They can be accessed through the following code snippet:

```
import sys
for p in sys.path :
    print(p)
```

(g) What does the content of **sys.path** signify? What does the order of contents of **sys.path** signify?

Answer

The **sys.path** variable contains a list of directories. The first directory in the list is the directory from where the current script has been executed. This is followed by a list of directories as specified in **PYTHONPATH** environment variable.

The modules being used in the program will be searched in the same order as the order of directories in the list.

(h) Where is the list of third-party packages maintained?

Answer

PyPI maintains a list of third-party packages.

(i) Which tool is commonly used for installing third-party packages?

Answer

pip is a commonly used tool for installing third-party packages.

(j) Do the following import statements serve the same purpose?

```
# version 1
import a, b, c, d

# version 2
import a
import b
import c
import d

# version 3
from a import *
from b import *
from c import *
from d import *
```

Answer

Yes

[C] State whether the following statements are True or False:

(a) A function can belong to a module and the module can belong to a package.

Answer

True

(b) A package can contain one or more modules in it.

Answer

True

(c) Nested packages are allowed.

Answer

True

(d) Contents of **sys.path** variable cannot be modified.

Answer

False

(e) In the statement **import a.b.c**, **c** cannot be a function.

Answer

True

(f) It is a good idea to use * to import all the functions/classes defined in a module.

Answer

True

17 Namespaces

Let Us Python Solutions

7th Edition

[A] State whether the following statements are True or False:

(a) Symbol table consists of information about each identifier used in our program.

Answer

True

(b) An identifier with global scope can be used anywhere in the program.

Answer

True

(c) It is possible to define a function within another function.

Answer

True

(d) If a function is nested inside another function, then variables defined in outer function are available to inner function.

Answer

True

(e) If nested functions create two variables with same name, then the two variables are treated as same variable.

Answer

False

(f) An inner function can be called from outside the outer function.

Answer

False

(g) If a function creates a variable by the same name as the one that exists in global scope, the function's variable will shadow out the global variable.

Answer

True

(h) Variables defined at global scope are available to all the functions defined in the program.

Answer

True

[B] Answer the following questions:

(a) What is the difference between the function **locals( )** and **globals( )**?

Answer

locals( ) - When called from a function/method, it returns a dictionary of identifiers that are accessible from that function/method.

globals( ) - When called from a function/method, it returns a dictionary of global identifiers that can be accessible from that function/method.

(b) Would the output of the following print statements be the same or different?

```
a = 20
b = 40
print(globals( ))
print(locals( ))
```

Answer

Output will be the same.

(c) Which different scopes can an identifier have?

Answer

Local(L), Enclosing(E), Global(G), Built-in(B).

(d) Which is the most liberal scope that an identifier can have?

Answer

Global scope is the most liberal scope that an identifier can have.

18 Classes and Objects

Let Us Python Solutions

7th Edition

[A] State whether the following statements are True or False:

(a) Class attributes and object attributes are same.

Answer

False

(b) A class data member is useful when all objects of the same class must share a common item of information.

Answer

True

(c) If a class has a data member and three objects are created from this class, then each object would have its own data member.

Answer

True

(d) A class can have class data as well as class methods.

Answer

True

(e) Usually, data in a class is kept private and the data is accessed / manipulated through object methods of the class.

Answer

True

(f) Member functions of an object have to be called explicitly, whereas, the **__init__( )** method gets called automatically.

Answer

True

(g) A constructor gets called whenever an object gets instantiated.

Answer

True

(h) The **__init__( )** method never returns a value.

Answer

True

(i) When an object goes out of scope, its **__del__( )** method gets called automatically.

Answer

True

(j) The **self** variable always contains the address of the object using which the method/data is being accessed.

Answer

True

(k) The **self** variable can be used even outside the class.

Answer

False

(l) The __init__( ) method gets called only once during the lifetime of an object.

Answer

True

(m) By default, instance data and methods in a class are public.

Answer

True

(n) In a class 2 constructors can coexist—a 0-argument constructor and a 2-argument constructor.

Answer

True

[B] Answer the following questions:

(a) Which methods in a class act as constructor?

Answer

__init__( ) in a class acts as a constructor.

(b) How many objects are created in the following code snippet?

```
a = 10
b = a
c = b
```

Answer

One object is created in the above code snippet.

(c) What is the difference between variables, **age** and **_age**?

Answer

age is a public attribute but **_age** is a private attribute of an object.

(d) What is the difference between the function **vars( )** and **dir( )**?

Answer

vars( ) - Returns a dictionary of attributes and their values.
dir( ) - Returns a list of attributes.

(e) In the following code snippet what is the difference between **display( )** and **show( )**?

```
class Message :
    def display(self, msg) :
        pass
    def show(msg) :
        pass
```

Answer

display( ) is an object method as it receives the address of the object (in **self)** using which it is called. **show( )** is class method and it can be called independent of an object.

(f) In the following code snippet what is the difference between **display( )** and **show( )**?

```
m = Message( )
m.display('Hi and Bye' )
Message.show('Hi and Bye' )
```

Answer

display( ) is an object method as it is being called using the object **m**. **show( )** is class method and it is being called using the class **Message**.

(g) How many parameters are being passed to **display( )** in the following code snippet:

```
m = Sample( )
m.display(10, 20, 30)
```

Answer

Four. Apart from 10, 20, 30, address of the object contained in **m** also gets passed to **display( )**.

[C] Attempt the following questions:

(a) Write a program to create a class that represents Complex numbers containing real and imaginary parts and then use it to perform complex number addition, subtraction, multiplication and division.

Program

```
import math

class Complex( ) :
    def __init__(self, x, y) :
        self.real = x
        self.imag = y
```

```
def display(self) :
    if self.imag < 0 :
        print(self.real, self.imag, 'i')
    else :
        print(self.real, '+', self.imag, 'i')

def add(self, x) :
    r = self.real + x.real
    i = self.imag + x.imag
    return Complex(r, i)

def subtract(self, x) :
    r = self.real - x.real
    i = self.imag - x.imag
    return Complex(r, i)

def multiply(self, x) :
    r = self.real * x.real - self.imag * x.imag
    i = self.real * x.imag + self.imag * x.real
    return Complex(r, i)

def conj(self) :
    r = self.real
    i = -self.imag
    return Complex(r, i)

def mods(self) :
    mod2 = self.real * self.real + self.imag * self.imag
    return math.sqrt(mod2)

def divide(self, x) :
    m = x.mods( )
    c = x.conj( )
    if m == 0 :
        print('Unable to divide the complex numbers')
    else :
        quo = self.multiply(c)
        quo.real = quo.real / m
        quo.imag = quo.imag / m
        return quo
```

```
a = Complex(2, 3)
b = Complex(6, -1)
print('a: ', end = '')
a.display( )
print('b: ', end = '')
b.display( )

c = a.add(b)
print('a + b = ', end = '')
c.display( )
d = a.subtract(b)
print('a - b = ', end = '')
d.display( )
e = a.multiply(b)
print('a * b = ', end = '')
e.display( )
f = a.divide ( b )
print('a / b = ', end = '')
f.display( )
```

Output

```
a: 2 + 3 i
b: 6 -1 i
a + b = 8 + 2 i
a - b = -4 + 4 i
a * b = 15 + 16 i
a / b = 1.4795908857482156 + 3.287979746107146 i
```

(b) Write a program that implements a **Matrix** class and performs addition, multiplication, and transpose operations on 3 x 3 matrices.

Program

```
class Matrix :
    size = 3
    def __init__(self, r, c) :
        self.rows = r
        self.cols = c
        self.arr = [ ]
```

```
def initializeMatrix(self) :
  print('Enter the contents of the matrix row-wise: ')

  for i in range(self.rows) :
    print('Row ', i, ':')
    a = [ ]
    for j in range(self.cols) :
      a.append(int(input( )))
    print('Row ', i, 'completed.')
    self.arr.append(a)
  print('Matrix initialized successfully.')

def displayMatrix(self) :
    for i in range(self.rows) :
        for j in range(self.cols) :
            print('{0:<5}'.format(self.arr[i][j]), end = '')
        print( )

def add(self, m) :
    mat = Matrix(self.rows, self.cols)
    for i in range(self.rows) :
        lst = [ ]
        for j in range(self.cols) :
            lst.append(self.arr[i][j] + m.arr[i][j])
        mat.arr.append(lst)
    return mat


def multiply(self, m) :
    mat = Matrix(self.rows, m.cols)
    for i in range(self.rows) :
        lst = [ ]
        for j in range(self.cols) :
            temp = 0
            for k in range(self.cols) :
                temp = temp + self.arr[i][k] * m.arr[k][j]
            lst.append(temp)
        mat.arr.append(lst)
    return mat

def transpose(self) :
```

```
        mat = Matrix(self.cols, self.rows)
        for i in range(self.cols) :
            lst = [ ]
            for j in range(self.rows) :
                lst.append(self.arr[j][i])
            mat.arr.append(lst)
        return mat

print('Initialize Matrix 1:')
mat1 = Matrix(3, 3)
mat1.initializeMatrix( )

print('Initialize Matrix 2:')
mat2 = Matrix(3, 3)
mat2.initializeMatrix( )

print('First Matrix: ')
mat1.displayMatrix( )

print('Second Matrix: ')
mat2.displayMatrix( )

mat3 = mat1.add(mat2)
print('After addition: ')
mat3.displayMatrix( )

mat4 = mat1.multiply(mat2)
print('After multiplication: ')
mat4.displayMatrix( )

mat5 = mat1.transpose( )
print('Transpose of Matrix 1: ')
mat5.displayMatrix( )
```

Output

```
Initialize Matrix 1:
Enter the contents of the matrix row-wise:
Row  0 :
1
2
3
```

```
Row 0 completed.
Row 1 :
1
2
3
Row 1 completed.
Row 2 :
1
2
3
Row 2 completed.
Matrix initialized successfully.
Initialize Matrix 2:
Enter the contents of the matrix row-wise:
Row 0 :
1
1
1
Row 0 completed.
Row 1 :
1
1
1
Row 1 completed.
Row 2 :
1
1
1
Row 2 completed.
Matrix initialized successfully.
First Matrix:
1 2 3
1 2 3
1 2 3
Second Matrix:
1 1 1
1 1 1
1 1 1
After addition:
2 3 4
2 3 4
```

```
2  3  4
After multiplication:
6  6  6
6  6  6
6  6  6
Transpose of Matrix 1:
1  1  1
2  2  2
3  3  3
```

(c) Write a program to create a class that can calculate the surface area and volume of a solid. The class should also have a provision to accept the data relevant to the solid.

Program

```
class Solid :
    def __init__(self, len_cbd = 0, br_cbd = 0, ht_cbd = 0, side_cube =
                        0, ht_cyl = 0, rad_cyl = 0, rad_sphere = 0) :
        self.len_cbd = len_cbd
        self.br_cbd = br_cbd
        self.ht_cbd = ht_cbd
        self.side_cube = side_cube
        self.ht_cyl = ht_cyl
        self.rad_cyl = rad_cyl
        self.rad_sphere = rad_sphere

    def sarea_cuboid(self) :
        sa = 2 * (self.len_cbd * self.br_cbd + self.len_cbd * self.ht_cbd
                    + self.ht_cbd * self.br_cbd)
        print('Surface area of cuboid is:', sa)

    def vol_cuboid(self) :
        v = self.len_cbd * self.br_cbd * self.ht_cbd
        print('Volume of cuboid is:', v)

    def sarea_cube(self) :
        sa = 6 * (self.side_cube * self.side_cube)
        print('Surface area of cube is:', sa)

    def vol_cube(self) :
        v =  self.side_cube * self.side_cube * self.side_cube
```

```
        print('Volume of cube is:', v)

    def sarea_cyl(self) :
        sa = 2 * (3.14 * self.rad_cyl * self.ht_cyl + 3.14 * self.rad_cyl
                * self.rad_cyl)
        print('Surface area of cylinder is:', sa)

    def vol_cyl(self) :
        v =  3.14 * self.rad_cyl * self.rad_cyl * self.ht_cyl
        print('Volume of cylinder is:', v)

    def sarea_sphere(self) :
        sa = 4 * (3.14 * self.rad_sphere * self.rad_sphere)
        print('Surface area of sphere is:', sa)

    def vol_sphere(self) :
        v =  4 / 3 * 3.14 * self.rad_sphere * self.rad_sphere
                * self.rad_sphere
        print('Volume of sphere is:', v)

choice = 1
while choice != 0 :
    print('1. Cuboid')
    print('2. Cube')
    print('3. Cylinder')
    print('4. Sphere')
    print('0. Exit')
    choice = int(input('Enter choice: '))

    if choice == 1 :
        l = int(input('Length of cuboid: '))
        b = int(input('Breadth of cuboid: '))
        h = int(input('Height of cuboid: '))
        s = Solid(len_cbd = l, br_cbd = b, ht_cbd = h)
        s.sarea_cuboid( )
        s.vol_cuboid( )

    elif choice == 2 :
        sd = int(input('Side of cube: '))
        s = Solid(side_cube = sd)
        s.sarea_cube( )
```

```
        s.vol_cube( )

    elif choice == 3 :
        h = int(input('Height of cylinder: '))
        r = int(input('Radius of base: '))
        s = Solid(rad_cyl = r, ht_cyl = h)
        s.sarea_cyl( )
        s.vol_cyl( )

    elif choice == 4 :
        r = int(input('Radius of sphere: '))
        s = Solid(rad_sphere = r)
        s.sarea_sphere( )
        s.vol_sphere( )

    elif choice == 0 :
        print('Exiting!')

    else :
        print('Invalid choice!!')
```

Output

```
1. Cuboid
2. Cube
3. Cylinder
4. Sphere
0. Exit
Enter choice: 1
Length of cuboid: 5
Breadth of cuboid: 4
Height of cuboid: 3
Surface area of cuboid is :  94
Volume of cuboid is :  60
1. Cuboid
2. Cube
3. Cylinder
4. Sphere
0. Exit
Enter choice: 2
Side of cube: 5
Surface area of cube is :  150
```

```
Volume of cube is :  125
1. Cuboid
2. Cube
3. Cylinder
4. Sphere
0. Exit
Enter choice: 3
Height of cylinder: 6
Radius of base: 3
Surface area of cylinder is :  169.56
Volume of cylinder is :  169.56
1. Cuboid
2. Cube
3. Cylinder
4. Sphere
0. Exit
Enter choice: 4
Radius of sphere: 6
Surface area of sphere is :  452.15999999999997
Volume of sphere is :  904.3199999999998
1. Cuboid
2. Cube
3. Cylinder
4. Sphere
0. Exit
Enter choice: 8
Invalid choice!!
1. Cuboid
2. Cube
3. Cylinder
4. Sphere
0. Exit
Enter choice: 0
Exiting!
```

(d) Write a program to create a class that can calculate the perimeter / circumference and area of a regular shape. The class should also have a provision to accept the data relevant to the shape.

Program

```
class Shape :
```

```
    def __init__(self, len_rect = 0, br_rect = 0, side_square = 0,
rad_cir = 0) :
        self.len_rect = len_rect
        self.br_rect = br_rect
        self.side_square = side_square
        self.rad_cir = rad_cir

    def area_rect(self) :
        a = self.len_rect * self.br_rect
        print('Area of rectangle is:', a)

    def peri_rect(self) :
        p = 2 * (self.len_rect + self.br_rect)
        print('Perimeter of rectangle is:', p)

    def area_square(self) :
        a = self.side_square * self.side_square
        print('Area of square is:', a)

    def peri_square(self) :
        p = 4 * self.side_square
        print('Perimeter of square is:', p)

    def area_cir(self) :
        a = 3.14 * self.rad_cir * self.rad_cir
        print('Area of cicle is:', a)

    def peri_cir(self) :
        p =  2 * 3.14 * self.rad_cir
        print('Perimeter of circle is:', p)

choice = 1
while choice != 0 :
    print('1. Rectangle')
    print('2. Square')
    print('3. Circle')
    print('0. Exit')
    choice = int(input('Enter choice: '))

    if choice == 1 :
        l = int(input('Length of rectangle: '))
```

```
        b = int(input('Breadth of rectangle: '))
        s = Shape(len_rect = l, br_rect = b)
        s.area_rect( )
        s.peri_rect( )

    elif choice == 2 :
        sd = int(input('Side of square: '))
        s = Shape(side_square = sd)
        s.area_square( )
        s.peri_square( )

    elif choice == 3 :
        r = int(input('Radius of circle: '))
        s = Shape(rad_cir = r)
        s.area_cir( )
        s.peri_cir( )

    elif choice == 0 :
        print('Exiting!')

    else :
        print('Invalid choice!!')
```

Output

```
1. Rectangle
2. Square
3. Circle
0. Exit
Enter choice: 1
Length of rectangle: 6
Breadth of rectangle: 5
Area of rectangle is: 30
Perimeter of rectangle is: 22
1. Rectangle
2. Square
3. Circle
0. Exit
Enter choice: 2
Side of square: 4
Area of square is: 16
Perimeter of square is: 16
```

```
1. Rectangle
2. Square
3. Circle
0. Exit
Enter choice: 3
Radius of circle: 5
Area of cicle is: 78.5
Perimeter of circle is: 31.400000000000002
1. Rectangle
2. Square
3. Circle
0. Exit
Enter choice: 5
Invalid choice!!
1. Rectangle
2. Square
3. Circle
0. Exit
Enter choice: 0
Exiting!
```

(e) Write a program that creates and uses a **Time** class to perform various time arithmetic operations.

Program

```
class Time :
    def __init__(self, hr = 0, mnt = 0, sec  = 0) :
        self.hours = hr
        self.minutes = mnt
        self.seconds  = sec

    def add_seconds(self, sec) :
        if sec > 86400 :
                return 1

        h = int(sec / 3600)
        m = int((sec - h * 3600) / 60)
        s = int((sec - h * 3600 - m * 60))

        self.hours = self.hours + h
        self.minutes = self.minutes + m
```

```
        self.seconds = self.seconds + s
        if self.seconds >= 60 :
            self.minutes += 1
            self.seconds -= 60
        if self.minutes >= 60 :
            self.hours += 1
            self.minute -= 60
        if self.hours >= 24 :
            self.hours = self.hours % 24

    def sub_seconds(self, sec) :
        if sec > 86400 :
            return 1

        h = int(sec / 3600)
        m = int((sec - h * 3600) / 60)
        s = int((sec - h * 3600 - m * 60))

        self.hours = self.hours - h
        self.minutes = self.minutes - m
        self.seconds = self.seconds - s
        if self.seconds < 0 :
            self.minutes -= 1
            self.seconds = 60 + self.seconds
        if self.minutes < 0 :
            self.hours -= 1
            self.minutes = 60 + self.minutes
        if self.hours < 0 :
            self.hours = 24 + self.hours

    def display(self) :
        print(self.hours, ':', self.minutes, ':', self.seconds)

t1 = Time(10, 15, 35)
print('Original time = ', end ='')
t1.display( )
val = t1.add_seconds(144)
if val == 1 :
    print('Cannot add more than 24 hours')
else :
    print('Time after adding 144 seconds = ', end ='')
```

```
    t1.display( )

print('Original time = ', end ='')
t1.display( )
val = t1.add_seconds(4000)
if val == 1 :
    print('Cannot add more than 24 hours')
else :
    print('Time after adding 4000 seconds = ', end ='')
    t1.display( )

print('Original time = ', end ='')
t1.display( )
val = t1.sub_seconds(4000)
if val == 1 :
    print('Cannot deduct more than 24 hours')
else :
    print('Time after deducting 4000 seconds = ', end ='')
    t1.display( )

print('Original time = ', end ='')
t1.display( )
val = t1.sub_seconds(144)
if val == 1 :
    print('Cannot deduct more than 24 hours')
else :
    print('Time after deducting 144 seconds = ', end ='')
    t1.display( )
```

Output

```
Original time = 10 : 15 : 35
Time after adding 144 seconds = 10 : 17 : 59
Original time = 10 : 17 : 59
Time after adding 4000 seconds = 11 : 24 : 39
Original time = 11 : 24 : 39
Time after deducting 4000 seconds = 10 : 17 : 59
Original time = 10 : 17 : 59
Time after deducting 144 seconds = 10 : 15 : 35
```

(f) Write a program to implement a linked list data structure by creating a linked list class. Each node in the linked list should contain the name of the car, its price and a link to the next node.

Program

```
class Node:
    def __init__(self, car, price):
        self.car = car
        self.price = price
        self.next = None

class LinkedList:
    def __init__(self):
        self.head = None

    def add(self, c, pr):
        n = Node(c, pr)
        if self.head is None :
            self.head = n
        else :
            p = self.head
            while p.next is not None :
                p = p.next

            p.next = n

    def display(self):
        p = self.head
        while p is not None:
            print(p.car, p.price)
            p = p.next

llst = LinkedList( )
llst.add('BMW', '55 lac')
llst.add('Honda City', '12 lac')
llst.add('Mercedes', '75 lac')
llst.add('Esteem', '10 lac')
llst.add('i20', '6 lac')
llst.add('i10', '4 lac')
llst.display( )
```

Output

BMW 55 lac
Honda City 12 lac
Mercedes 75 lac
Esteem 10 lac
i20 6 lac
i10 4 lac

[D] Match the following:

a. dir( )	1. Nested packages
b. vars( )	2. Identifiers, their type & scope
c. Variables in a function	3. Returns dictionary
d. import a.b.c	4. Local namespace
e. Symbol table	5. Returns list
f. Variables outside all functions	6. Global namespace

Answer

dir( ) - Returns list
vars( ) - Returns dictionary
Variables in a function - Local namespace
import a.b.c - Nested packages
Symbol table - Identifiers, their type & scope
Variables outside all functions - Global namespace

19 Intricacies of Classes & Objects

Let Us Python Solutions

7th Edition

[A] State whether the following statements are True or False:

(a) A global function can call a class method as well as an instance method.

Answer

True

(b) In Python a function, class, method and module are treated as objects.

Answer

True

(c) Given an object, it is possible to determine its type and address.

Answer

True

(d) It is possible to delete attributes of an object during execution of the program.

Answer

True

(e) Arithmetic operators, Comparison operators and Compound assignment operators can be overloaded in Python.

Answer

True

(f) The + operator has been overloaded in the classes **str**, **list** and **int**.

Answer

False

[B] Answer the following questions:

(a) Which functions should be defined to overload the +, -, / and // operators?

Answer

```
+   __add__(self, other)
-   __sub__(self, other)
/   __truediv__(self, other)
//  __floordiv__(self, other)
```

(b) How many objects are created by **lst = [10, 10, 10, 30]**?

Answer

Two objects are created, one which refers to 10 and another which refers to 30. This can be verified as follows:

```
lst = [10, 10, 10, 30]
print(id(lst[ 0 ]), id(lst[ 1 ]), id(lst[ 2 ]), id(lst[ 3 ]))
```

Its output will be:

```
1481758656 1481758656 1481758656 1481758976
```

(c) How will you define a structure **Employee** containing the attributes Name, Age, Salary, Address, Hobbies dynamically?

Answer

```
class Employee:
    pass
e = Employee( )
e.name = 'Rohan'
e.age = 29
e.salary = 340000
e.address = 'xyz'
e.hobbies = 'painting'
```

(d) To overload the + operator, which method should be defined in the corresponding class?

Answer

```
__add__(self, other)
```

(e) To overload the % operator, which method should be defined in the corresponding class?

Answer

__mod__(self, other)

(f) To overload the //= operator, which method should be defined in the corresponding class?

Answer

__ifloordiv__(self, other)

(g) If a class contains instance methods **__ge__( )** and **__ne__( )**, what do they signify?

Answer

They represent overloaded >= and != methods.

(h) What conclusion can be drawn if the following statements work?

```
a = (10, 20) + (30, 40)
b = 'Good' + 'Morning'
c = [10, 20, 30] + [40, 50, 60]
```

Answer

+ operator has been overloaded in **tuple**, **str** and **list** class.

(i) What will be the output of the following code snippet?

```
a = (10, 20) - (30, 40)
b = 'Good' - 'Morning'
c = [10, 20, 30] - [40, 50, 60]
```

Answer

Error: - operator has not been overloaded in **tuple**, **str** or **list** class.

(j) Will the following statement work? What is your conclusion if it works?

```
print ( 'Hello' * 7)
```

Answer

Yes, it will. It will output Hello 7 times. We can conclude that * operator has been overloaded in **str** class.

(k) Which out of +, - and * have been overloaded in **str** class?

Answer

+ and * have been overloaded in **str** class.

(l) When would the method **__truediv__( )** defined in the Sample class shown below would get called?

```
class Sample :
    def __truediv__(self, other) :
        pass
```

Answer

When / operator is used on **Sample** objects.

(m) If **!=** operator has been overloaded in a class then the expression **c1 <= c2** would get converted into which function call?

Answer

A call to function **__le__( )**.

(n) How will you define the overloaded * operator for the following code snippet?

```
c1 = Complex(1.1, 0.2)
c2 = Complex(1.1, 0.2)
c3 = c1 * c2
```

Answer

```
class Complex :
    def __init__(self, x, y) :
        self.real = x
        self.imag = y

    def display(self) :
        if self.imag < 0 :
```

```
            print(self.real, self.imag, 'i')
        else :
            print(self.real, '+', self.imag, 'i')

    def __mul__(self, other) :
        r = self.real * other.real - self.imag * other.imag
        i = self.real * other.imag + self.imag * other.real
        return Complex(r, i)

a = Complex(2, 3)
b = Complex(6, -1)
c = a * b
c.display( )
```

(o) Implement a **String** class containing the following functions:

- Overloaded += operator function to perform string concatenation.
- Method **toLower( )** to convert upper case letters to lower case.
- Method **toUpper( )** to convert lower case letters to upper case.

Answer

```
class String :
    def __init__(self, x) :
        self.s = x

    def display(self) :
        print(self.s)

    def __iadd__(self, other) :
        self.s = self.s + other.s
        return self

    def toUpper(self) :
        self.s = self.s.upper( )

    def toLower(self) :
        self.s = self.s.lower( )

a = String('www.ykanetkar')
b = String('.com')
```

```
a += b
a.display( )
a.toUpper( )
a.display( )
a.toLower( )
a.display( )
```

[C] Match the following:

a. Can't use as identifier name	1. class name
b. basic_salary	2. class variable
c. CellPhone	3. keyword
d. count	4. local variable in a function
e. self	5. private variable
f. _fuel_used	6. strongly private identifier
g. __draw( )	7. method that Python calls
h. __iter__( )	8. meaningful only in instance func.

Answer

Can't use as identifier name - keyword
basic_salary - class variable
CellPhone - class name
count - local variable in a function
self - meaningful only in instance function
_fuel_used - private variable
__draw( ) - strongly private identifier
__iter__( ) - method that Python calls

20 Containership and Inheritance

Let Us Python Solutions

7th Edition

[A] State whether the following statements are True or False:

(a) Inheritance is the ability of a class to inherit properties and behavior from a parent class by extending it.

Answer

True

(b) Containership is the ability of a class to contain objects of different classes as member data.

Answer

True

(c) We can derive a class from a base class even if the base class's source code is not available.

Answer

True

(d) Multiple inheritance is different from multiple levels of inheritance.

Answer

True

(e) An object of a derived class cannot access members of base class if the member names begin with __.

Answer

True

(f) Creating a derived class from a base class requires fundamental changes to the base class.

Answer

False

(g) If a base class contains a member function **func( )**, and a derived class does not contain a function with this name, an object of the derived class cannot access **func( )**.

Answer

False

(h) If no constructors are specified for a derived class, objects of the derived class will use the constructors in the base class.

Answer

False

(i) If a base class and a derived class each include a member function with the same name, the member function of the derived class will be called by an object of the derived class.

Answer

True

(j) A class **D** can be derived from class **C**, which is derived from class **B**, which is derived from class **A**.

Answer

True

(k) It is illegal to make objects of one class members of another class.

Answer

False

[B] Answer the following:

(a) Which module should be imported to create abstract class?

Answer

abc

(b) For a class to be abstract from which class should we inherit it?

Answer

ABC

(c) Suppose there is a base class **B** and a derived class **D** derived from **B**. **B** has two **public** member functions **b1( )** and **b2( )**, whereas **D** has two member functions **d1( )** and **d2( )**. Write these classes for the following different situations:

- **b1( )** should be accessible from main module, **b2( )** should not be.
- Neither **b1( )**, nor **b2( )** should be accessible from main module.
- Both **b1( )** and **b2( )** should be accessible from main module.

Program

```
# Version 1: b1( ) accessible, b2( ) inaccessible
class B :
    def b1(self) :
        print('B - b1')

    def __b2(self) :
        print('B - b2')

class D(B) :
    def d1(self) :
        print('D - d1')

    def d2(self) :
        print('D - d2')

b = B( )
b.b1( )      # works
b.__b2( )  # error


# Version 2: b1( ) inaccessible, b2( ) inaccessible
class B :
    def __b1(self) :
        print('B - b1')

    def __b2(self) :
        print('B - b2')
```

```
class D(B) :
    def d1(self) :
        print('D - d1')

    def d2(self) :
        print('D - d2')

b = B( )
b.__b1( )  # error
b.__b2( )  # error


# Version 3: b1( ) accessible, b2( ) accessible
class B :
    def b1(self) :
        print('B - b1')

    def b2(self) :
        print('B - b2')

class D(B) :
    def d1(self) :
        print('D - d1')

    def d2(self) :
        print('D - d2')

b = B( )
b.b1( )     # works
b.b2( )     # works
```

(d) If a class **D** is derived from two base classes **B1** and **B2**, then write these classes each containing a constructor. Ensure that while building an object of type **D**, the constructor of **B2** should get called. Also provide a destructor in each class. In what order would these destructors get called?

Program

```
class B1 :
    def __init__(self) :
```

```
        print('B1 Ctor')

    def __del__(self) :
        print('B1 Dtor')

class B2 :
    def __init__(self) :
        print('B2 Ctor')

    def __del__(self) :
        print('B2 Dtor')

class D(B1, B2) :
    def __init__(self) :
        B2.__init__(self)
        print('D Ctor')

    def __del__(self) :
        B1.__del__(self)
        B2.__del__(self)
        print('D Dtor')

d = D( )
d = None
```

Output

```
B2 Ctor
D Ctor
B1 Dtor
B2 Dtor
D Dtor
```

The destructors of base classes get called before destructor of derived class.

(e) Create an abstract class called **Vehicle** containing methods **speed( )**, **maintenance( )** and **value( )** in it. Derive classes **FourWheeler**, **TwoWheeler** and **Airborne** from **Vehicle** class. Check whether you can prevent creation of objects of **Vehicle** class. Call the methods using objects of other classes.

Program

```
from abc import ABC, abstractmethod
class Vehicle(ABC) :
    @abstractmethod
    def speed(self) :
        pass

    def maintenance(self) :
        pass

    def value(self) :
        pass

class FourWheeler(Vehicle) :
    def speed(self) :
        print('In FourWheeler.speed')

    def maintenance(self) :
        print('In FourWheeler.maintenance')

    def value(self) :
        print('In FourWheeler.value')

class TwoWheeler(Vehicle) :
    def speed(self) :
        print('In TwoWheeler.speed')

    def maintenance(self) :
        print('In TwoWheeler.maintenance')

    def value(self) :
        print('In TwoWheeler.value')

# v = Vehicle( )  # will result in error, as Vehicle is abstract class

fw = FourWheeler( )
fw.speed( )
fw.maintenance( )
fw.value( )

tw = TwoWheeler( )
```

```
tw.speed( )
tw.maintenance( )
tw.value( )
```

Output

```
In FourWheeler.speed
In FourWheeler.maintenance
In FourWheeler.value
In TwoWheeler.speed
In TwoWheeler.maintenance
In TwoWheeler.value
```

(f) Assume a class **D** that is derived from class **B**. Which of the following can an object of class **D** access?

- members of **D**
- members of **B**

Answer

Both

[C] Match the following:

a. __mro__( )	1. 'has a' relationship
b. Inheritance	2. Object creation not allowed
c. __var	3. Super class
d. Abstract class	4. Root class
e. Parent class	5. 'is a' relationship
f. object	6. Name mangling
g. Child class	7. Decides resolution order
h. Containership	8. Sub class

Answer

__mro__( ) - Decides resolution order
Inheritance - 'is a' relationship
__var - Name mangling
Abstract class - Object creation not allowed
Parent class - Super class
object - Root class
Child class - Sub class
Containership - 'has a' relationship

[D] Attempt the following questions:

(a) From which class is any abstract class derived?

Answer

ABC

(b) At a time, a class can be derived from how many abstract classes?

Answer

Any number

(c) How do we create an abstract class in Python?

Answer

By deriving it from **ABC** class of **abc** module as shown below:

```
from abc import ABC
class Sample(ABC) :
    pass
```

(d) What can an abstract class contain—instance method, class method, abstract method?

Answer

All three.

(e) How many objects can be created from an abstract class?

Answer

Zero

(f) What will happen on execution of this code snippet?

```
from abc import ABC, abstractmethod
class Sample(ABC) :
@abstractmethod
def display(self) :
    pass
s = Sample( )
```

Answer

Error: Cannot create an object from an abstract class.

(g) Suppose there is a class called **Vehicle**. What should be done to ensure that an object should not be created from **Vehicle** class?

Answer

Make it an abstract class by deriving it from class **ABC** of **abc** module.

(h) How will you mark an instance method in an abstract class as abstract?

Answer

My marking it with the decorator **@abstractmethod**.

(i) There is something wrong in the following code snippet. How will you rectify it?

```
class Shape(ABC) :
@abstractmethod
def draw(self) :
    pass

class Circle(Shape) :
@abstractmethod
def draw(self) :
    print('In draw')
```

Answer

Both **draw( )** methods and their decorators must be indented.

21 Iterators and Generators

Let Us Python Solutions

7th Edition

[A] Answer the following questions:

(a) Write a program to create a list of 5 odd integers. Replace the third element with a list of 4 even integers. Flatten, sort and print the list.

Program

```
lst = [1, 3, 9, 13, 17]
lst[2] = [2, 8, 12, 16]
lst1 = [ ]
for num in lst[2] :
    lst1.append(num)
lst = lst[0:2] + lst1 + lst[3:]
print(lst)
```

Output

```
[1, 3, 2, 8, 12, 16, 13, 17]
```

(b) Write a program to flatten the following list:

mat1 = [[1, 2, 3, 4], [5, 6, 7, 8], [9, 10, 11, 12]]

Program

```
lst = [ ]
mat1 = [[1, 2, 3, 4], [5, 6, 7, 8], [9, 10, 11, 12]]
lst = [ ]
for m in mat1 :
    for ele in m :
        lst.append(ele)
print(lst)
```

Output

```
[1, 2, 3, 4, 5, 6, 7, 8, 9, 10, 11, 12]
```

(c) Write a program to generate a list of numbers in the range 2 to 50 that are divisible by 2 and 4.

Program

```
lst = [n for n in range(2, 50) if n % 2 == 0 and n % 4 == 0]
print(lst)
```

Output

```
[4, 8, 12, 16, 20, 24, 28, 32, 36, 40, 44, 48]
```

(d) Suppose there are two lists, each holding 5 strings. Write a program to generate a list that consists of strings that are concatenated by picking corresponding elements from the two lists.

Program

```
lst1 = ['Cat', 'Dog', 'Lion', 'Tiger']
lst2 = ['Lily', 'Rose', 'Hibiscus', 'Lavender']
loft = zip(lst1, lst2)
lst3 = [ ]
for tpl in loft :
    lst3.append(tpl[0] + tpl[1])
print(lst3)
```

Output

```
['CatLily', 'DogRose', 'LionHibiscus', 'TigerLavender']
```

(e) Suppose a list contains 20 integers generated randomly. Receive a number from the keyboard and report position of all occurrences of this number in the list.

Program

```
import random
lst =[int(10 * random.random( )) for n in range(20)]
print(lst)
num = int(input('Enter number between 1 to 10: '))
indexlist = [i for i in range(len(lst)) if lst[i] == num]
print(num, 'is present at following positions')
print(indexlist)
```

Output

```
[2, 8, 1, 6, 0, 6, 4, 4, 4, 8, 6, 9, 1, 2, 5, 0, 1, 4, 8, 8]
Enter number between 1 to 10: 4
4 is present at following positions
[6, 7, 8, 17]
```

(f) Suppose there are two lists—one contains questions, and another contains lists of 4 possible answers for each question. Write a program to generate a list that contains lists of question and its 4 possible answers.

Program

```
qlist = ['What is capital of India', 'Which is your favorite color?']
alist = [['Delhi', 'Mumbai', 'Hyderabad', 'Bangalore'], ['Red', 'Blue',
'White', 'Black']]
qalist = [ ]
for q, a in zip(qlist, alist) :
    lst = [q, *a]
    qalist.append(lst)
print(qalist)
```

Output

```
[['What is capital of India', 'Delhi', 'Mumbai', 'Hyderabad',
'Bangalore'], ['Which is your favorite color?', 'Red', 'Blue', 'White',
'Black']]
```

(g) Suppose a list has 20 numbers. Write a program that removes all duplicates from this list.

Program

```
lst =[1, 1, 1, 1, 1, 2, 2, 2, 3, 1, 4, 1, 3, 2, 1, 1, 2, 2, 5, 5]
lst = list(set(lst))
print(lst)
```

Output

```
[1, 2, 3, 4, 5]
```

(h) Write a program to obtain a median value of a list of numbers, without disturbing the order of the numbers in the list.

Program

```
lst1 = [1, 2, 3, 4, 5, 6]
n = len(lst1)
s = sorted(lst1)
m = (sum(s[n // 2 - 1 : n // 2 + 1]) / 2.0, s[n // 2])[n % 2]
```

```
print(m)

lst2 = [7, 6, 5, 4, 3, 2, 1]
n = len(lst2)
s = sorted(lst2)
m = (sum(s[n // 2 - 1 : n // 2 + 1]) / 2.0, s[n // 2])[n % 2]
print(m)
```

Output

```
3.5
4
```

(i) A list contains only positive and negative integers. Write a program to obtain the number of negative numbers present in the list.

Program

```
lst1 = [-1, -2, -3, 1, 2, 3]
lst2 = [n for n in lst1 if n < 0]
c = len(lst2)
print(c)
```

Output

```
3
```

(j) Write a program to convert a list of tuples

[(10, 20, 30), (150.55, 145.60, 157.65), ('A1', 'B1', 'C1')]

into a list

[(10, 150.55, 'A1'), (20, 145.60, 'B1'), (30, 157.65, 'C1')]

Program

```
lst = [(10, 20, 30), (150.55, 145.60, 157.65), ('A1', 'B1', 'C1')]
lst1 = [ ]
for a, b, c in zip(*lst) :
    lst1.append((a, b, c))
print(lst1)
```

Output

```
[(10, 150.55, 'A1'), (20, 145.6, 'B1'), (30, 157.65, 'C1')]
```

(k) What will be the output of the following program?

```
x = [[1, 2, 3, 4], [4, 5, 6, 7]]
y = [[1, 1], [2, 2], [3, 3], [4, 4]]
l1 = [xrow for xrow in x]
print(l1)
l2 = [(xrow, ycol) for ycol in zip(*y) for xrow in x]
print(l2)
```

Output

```
[[1, 2, 3, 4], [4, 5, 6, 7]]
[([1, 2, 3, 4], (1, 2, 3, 4)), ([4, 5, 6, 7], (1, 2, 3, 4)), ([1, 2, 3, 4], (1, 2, 3,
4)), ([4, 5, 6, 7], (1, 2, 3, 4))]
```

(l) Write a program that uses a generator to create a set of unique words from a line input through the keyboard.

Program

```
line = input('Enter a sentence: ')
s = set(line.split( ))
print(s)
```

Output

```
Enter a sentence: I did not do this. He did it or she did it
{'it', 'or', 'do', 'He', 'she', 'did', 'this.', 'I', 'not'}
```

(m) Write a program that uses a generator to find out maximum marks obtained by a student and his name from tuples of multiple students.

Program

```
def getname(stud, mm) :
    if stud[1] == mm :
        return stud[0]

lst = [('Ajay', 45), ('Sujay', 55), ('Nirmal', 40), ('Vijay', 75)]
```

```
maxmarks = max(student[1] for student in lst)
for student in lst :
    name = getname(student, maxmarks)
print(name, maxmarks )
```

Output

```
Vijay 75
```

(n) Write a program that uses a generator that generates characters from a string in reverse order.

Program

```
n = 'Sacchidanand'
revn = [ch for ch in n[::-1]]
print(revn)
```

Output

```
['d', 'n', 'a', 'n', 'a', 'd', 'i', 'h', 'c', 'c', 'a', 'S']
```

(o) What is the difference between the following statements?

```
sum([x**2 for x in range(20)])
sum(x**2 for x in range(20))
```

Answer

The first expression first generates a list and then obtains the sum of all elements in the list.

The second expression keeps a running sum of square of each number generates as and when they get generated.

Both will yield the same result, but the second one is more efficient as it occupies less space.

(p) Suppose there are two lists, each holding 5 strings. Write a program to generate a list that consists of strings that are concatenated by picking corresponding elements from the two lists.

Program

```
lst1 = ['Cat', 'Dog', 'Lion', 'Tiger']
```

```
lst2 = ['Lily', 'Rose', 'Hibiscus', 'Lavender']
lst3 = [(x + y) for x, y in zip(lst1, lst2)]
print(lst3)
```

Output

```
['CatLily', 'DogRose', 'LionHibiscus', 'TigerLavender']
```

(q) 36 unique combinations can result from the use of two dice. Create a dictionary which stores these combinations as tuples.

Program

```
lst = [(d1, d2) for d1 in range(1,7) for d2 in range(1,7)]
print(lst)
```

Output

```
[(1, 1), (1, 2), (1, 3), (1, 4), (1, 5), (1, 6), (2, 1), (2, 2), (2, 3), (2, 4), (2,
5), (2, 6), (3, 1), (3, 2), (3, 3), (3, 4), (3, 5), (3, 6), (4, 1), (4, 2), (4, 3),
(4, 4), (4, 5), (4, 6), (5, 1), (5, 2), (5, 3), (5, 4), (5, 5), (5, 6), (6, 1), (6,
2), (6, 3), (6, 4), (6, 5), (6, 6)]
```

22 Exception Handling

Let Us Python Solutions

7th Edition

[A] State whether the following statements are True or False:

(a) The exception handling mechanism is supposed to handle compile time errors.

Answer

False

(b) It is necessary to declare the exception class within the class in which an exception is going to be thrown.

Answer

False

(c) Every raised exception must be caught.

Answer

True

(d) For one **try** block there can be multiple **except** blocks.

Answer

True

(e) When an exception is raised, an exception class's constructor gets called.

Answer

True

(f) **try** blocks cannot be nested.

Answer

False

(g) Proper destruction of an object is guaranteed by exception handling mechanism.

Answer

False

(h) All exceptions occur at runtime.

Answer

True

(i) Exceptions offer an object-oriented way of handling runtime errors.

Answer

True

(j) If an exception occurs, then the program terminates abruptly without getting any chance to recover from the exception.

Answer

False

(k) No matter whether an exception occurs or not, the statements in the **finally** clause (if present) will get executed.

Answer

True

(l) A program can contain multiple **finally** clauses.

Answer

False

(m) **finally** clause is used to perform cleanup operations like closing the network/database connections.

Answer

True

(n) While raising a user-defined exception, multiple values can be set in the exception object.

Answer

True

(o) In one function/method, there can be only one **try** block.

Answer

False

(p) An exception must be caught in the same function/method in which it is raised.

Answer

False

(q) All values set up in the exception object are available in the **except** block that catches the exception.

Answer

True

(r) If our program does not catch an exception, then Python runtime catches it.

Answer

True

(s) It is possible to create user-defined exceptions.

Answer

True

(t) All types of exceptions can be caught using the **Exception** class.

Answer

True

(u) For every **try** block there must be a corresponding **finally** block.

Answer

False

[B] Answer the following:

(a) If we do not catch the exception thrown at runtime then who catches it?

Answer

If we do not catch the exception thrown at runtime then Python runtime catches it.

(b) Explain in short, the most compelling reasons for using exception handling over conventional error handling approaches.

Answer

Given below are the reasons for preferring exception handling over conventional error handling:

- It allows separation of program's logic from error handling logic making it more reliable and maintainable.

- Propagation of exception information from the place where an exception occurred to the place where it is tackled is done by runtime environment and is not the programmer's responsibility.

- It allows guaranteed cleanup in the event of runtime errors.

(c) Is it necessary that all classes that can be used to represent exceptions be derived from base class **Exception**?

Answer

Yes

(d) What is the use of **finally** block in Python exception handling mechanism?

Answer

Cleanup activities like releasing external resources, network connections or database connections etc. is done in the finally block since it gets called irrespective of whether an exception occurred or not.

(e) How does nested exception handling work in Python?

Answer

If an exception is raised in the nested try block, the nested except block is used to handle it. If it does not, then the outer except blocks are used to handle the exception.

(f) Write a program that receives 10 integers and stores them and their cubes in a dictionary. If the number entered is less than 3, raise a user-defined exception **NumberTooSmall**, and if the number entered is more than 30, then raise a user-defined exception **NumberTooBig**. Whether an exception occurs or not, at the end print the contents of the dictionary.

Program

```
class NumberTooSmall(Exception) :
    def __init__(self, num) :
        self.num = num

    def get_details(self) :
        return {'Number too small' : self.num}

class NumberTooBig(Exception) :
    def __init__(self, num) :
        self.num = num

    def get_details(self) :
        return {'Number too big' : self.num}

class Numbers :
    def __init__(self) :
        self.dct = { }

    def append(self, num, cube ) :
```

```
        self.dct[num] = cube

    def display(self) :
        for k, v in self.dct.items( ) :
            print(k, v)
        print( )

n = Numbers( )
print('Enter 10 numbers between 3 to 30 :')
try :
    for x in range(10) :
        num = int(input( ))
        if num > 30 :
            raise NumberTooBig(num)
        elif num < 3 :
            raise NumberTooSmall(num)
        else :
            cube = num * num *num
            n.append(num, cube)
except NumberTooBig as ntb :
    print(ntb.get_details( ))
except NumberTooSmall as nts :
    print(nts.get_details( ))
finally :
    n.display( )
```

Output

```
Enter 10 numbers between 3 to 30 :
5
6
8
9
12
10
2
{'Number too small': 2}
5 125
6 216
8 512
9 729
12 1728
```

10 1000

(g) What is wrong with the following code snippet?

```
try :
    # some statements
except :
    # report error 1
except ZeroDivisionError :
    # report error 2
```

Answer

Empty except block must be the last except block.

(h) Which of these keywords is not part of Python's exception handling—**try, catch, throw, except, raise, finally, else**?

Answer

catch and **throw** are not part of Python's exception handling.

(i) What will be the output of the following code?

```
def fun( ) :
    try :
        return 10
    finally :
        return 20

k = fun( )
print(k)
```

Output

20

23 File Input/Output

Let Us Python Solutions

7th Edition

[A] State whether the following statements are True or False:

(a) If a file is opened for reading, it is necessary that the file must exist.

Answer

True

(b) If a file opened for writing already exists, its contents would be overwritten.

Answer

True

(c) For opening a file in append mode it is necessary that the file should exist.

Answer

False

[B] Answer the following questions:

(a) What sequence of activities take place on opening a file for reading in text mode?

Answer

On opening a file for reading in text mode the following activities are performed:

1. The disk is searched for the existence of the file.
2. The file is brought into memory.
3. A pointer is set up which points to the first character in the file.
4. All the above.

(b) Is it necessary that a file created in text mode must always be opened in text mode for subsequent operations?

Answer

Yes

(c) While using the statement,

fp = open('myfile', 'r')

what happens if,

- 'myfile' does not exist on the disk
- 'myfile' exists on the disk

Answer

The disk is searched for existence of the 'myfile'. If it does not exist, then **FileNotFoundError** exception is raised. If it exists it is brought into memory and a pointer is set up which points to the first character in the file.

(d) While using the statement,

```
f = open('myfile', 'wb')
```

what happens if,

- 'myfile' does not exist on the disk
- 'myfile' exists on the disk

Answer

The disk is searched for existence of the 'myfile'. If it does not exist, then **FileNotFoundError** exception is raised. If it exists it is brought into memory and a pointer is set up which points to the first byte in the file.

(e) A floating-point list contains percentage marks obtained by students in an examination. To store these marks in a file 'marks.dat', in which mode would you open the file and why?

Answer

'marks.dat' should be opened in 'wb' mode. This is because in binary mode when we store a number in a disk file, it occupies as many bytes as it occupies in memory. If file is opened in 'w' mode then the number is stored character by character and hence it would occupy as many bytes as the length of the number.

[C] Attempt the following questions:

(a) Write a program to read a file and display its contents along with line numbers before each line.

Program

```
# Display file contents
f = open('sample.txt', 'r')
while True :
   data = f.readline( )
   if data == '' :
      break
   print(data)
f.close( )
```

Output

```
CPython - is the reference implementation, written in C.
PyPy - Written in a subset of Python language called RPython.
Jython - Written in Java.
IronPython - Written in C#.
```

(b) Write a program to append the contents of one file at the end of another.

Program

```
# Append files
f1 = open('sample.txt', 'r')
para1 = ''
while True :
   data = f1.readline( )
   if data == '' :
      break
   para1 += data

f2 = open('trial.txt', 'r+')
para2 = ''
while True :
   data = f2.readline( )
   if data == '' :
      break
   para2 += data

para2 += para1
print(para2)
```

```
f2.seek(0, 0)
f2.write(para2)
f1.close( )
f2.close( )
```

Output

'sample.txt' contains a few lines in lower case. 'trial.txt. contains the same lines in uppercase. After concatenation the contents of 'tiral.txt' is as shown below:

CPYTHON - IS THE REFERENCE IMPLEMENTATION, WRITTEN IN C.
PYPY - WRITTEN IN A SUBSET OF PYTHON LANGUAGE CALLED RPYTHON.
JYTHON - WRITTEN IN JAVA.
IRONPYTHON - WRITTEN IN C#.
CPython - is the reference implementation, written in C.
PyPy - Written in a subset of Python language called RPython.
Jython - Written in Java.
IronPython - Written in C#.

(c) Suppose a file contains student's records with each record containing the name and age of a student. Write a program to read these records and display them in sorted order by name.

Program

```
# Sort records in a file
import operator
f = open('students.txt', 'r')
dct = { }
while True :
   data = f.readline( )
   if data == '' :
      break
   stud = data.split( )
   dct[stud[0]] = stud[1]

f.close( )
lst = sorted(dct.items( ), key = operator.itemgetter(0))
for item in lst :
   print(item[0], item[1])
```

Output

Anil 23
Prabhu 22
Rakesh 25
Sameer 30
Sanjay 25
Suresh 33

(d) Write a program to copy contents of one file to another. While doing so replace all lowercase characters with their equivalent uppercase characters.

Program

```
# Convert file contents to uppercase
f1 = open('stud1.txt', 'r')
f2 = open('stud2.txt', 'w')
while True :
    data = f1.readline( )
    if data == '' :
        break
    data = data.upper( )
    f2.write(data)

f1.close( )
f2.close( )
```

Output

SANJAY 25
SAMEER 30
ANIL 23
SURESH 33
PRABHU 22
RAKESH 25

(e) Write a program that merges lines alternately from two files and writes the results to a new file. If one file has a smaller number of lines than the other, the remaining lines from the larger file should be simply copied into the target file.

Program

```
# Merge two files alternating its lines
f1 = open('sample.txt', 'r')
f2 = open('trial.txt', 'r')
f3 = open('combined.txt', 'w')
while True :
    data1 = f1.readline( )
    if data1 == '' :
        break
    f3.write(data1)
    data2 = f2.readline( )
    if data2 == '' :
        break
    f3.write(data2)

if data1 != '' :
    while True :
        data1 = f1.readline( )
        if data1 == '' :
            break
        f3.write(data1)

if data2 != '' :
    while True :
        data2 = f2.readline( )
        if data2 == '' :
            break
        f3.write(data2)

f1.close( )
f2.close( )
f3.close( )
```

Output

File 'sample.txt' contains following lines:

1. SANJAY 25
2. SAMEER 30
3. ANIL 23
4. SURESH 33
5. PRABHU 22

6. DINESH 40
7. Suresh 34

File 'trial.txt' contains following lines:

1. Sandhya 25
2. Seema 30
3. Swati 23
4. Supriya 33
5. Sunidhi 22

Resulting file 'comined.txt' contains following lines:

1. SANJAY 25
1. Sandhya 25
2. SAMEER 30
2. Seema 30
3. ANIL 23
3. Swati 23
4. SURESH 33
4. Supriya 33
5. PRABHU 22
5. Sunidhi 22
6. DINESH 40
7. Suresh 34

(f) Suppose an Employee object contains following details:

employee code
employee name
date of joining
salary

Write a program to serialize and deserialize this data.

Program

```
# Serialization, Deserialization of employee record
import json
def encode_employee(x):
    if isinstance(x, Employee) :
        return(x.ecode, x.ename, x.doj, x.sal)
    else :
        raise TypeError('Complex object is not JSON serializable')
```

```
def decode_employee(dct):
  if '__Employee__' in dct :
    return Employee(dct['ecode'], dct['ename'], dct['doj'], dct['sal'])
  return dct

class Employee :
  def __init__(self, ecode, ename, doj, sal) :
    self.ecode = ecode
    self.ename = ename
    self.doj = doj
    self.sal = sal

  def print_data(self) :
    print(self.ecode, self.ename, self.doj, self.sal)

e = Employee('A101', 'Sameer', '17/11/2017', 25000)
f = open('data', 'w+')
json.dump(e, f, default = encode_employee)
f.seek(0)
ine = json.load(f, object_hook = decode_employee)
print(ine)
```

Output

```
['A101', 'Sameer', '17/11/2017', 25000]
```

(g) A hospital keeps a file of blood donors in which each record has the format:

Name: 20 Columns
Address: 40 Columns
Age: 2 Columns
Blood Type: 1 Column (Type 1, 2, 3 or 4)

Write a program to read the file and print a list of all blood donors whose age is below 25 and whose blood type is 2.

Program

```
# Formatted reading/writing
donors = {
            'Sanjay' : ['Gokulpeth', 25, 1],
            'Sunil' : ['Shankarnagar', 26, 2],
```

```
                'Akash' : ['Sitaburdi', 27, 3],
                'Rahul' : ['Ramnagar', 23, 2],
                'Riddhi' : ['Dharampeth', 22, 2],
                'Mangal' : ['Ramdaspeth', 21, 2]
            }
f = open('donors.txt', 'w+')
for k, v in donors.items( ) :
    s = '{0:20s}{1:40s}{2:2s}{3:1s}\n'.format(k, v[0], str(v[1]), str(v[2]))
    f.write(s)
f.seek(0,0)
while True :
    data = f.readline( )
    if data == '' :
        break
    nam = data[:20]
    address = data[20:59]
    age = int(data[60:62:])
    bloodtype = int(data[62:])
    if age < 25 and bloodtype == 2 :
        print(nam, address, age, bloodtype)
f.close( )
```

Output

```
Rahul        Ramnagar                  23 2
Riddhi       Dharampeth                22 2
Mangal       Ramdaspeth                21 2
```

(h) Given a list of names of students in a class, write a program to store the names in a file on disk. Make a provision to display the **n**th name in the list, where **n** is read from the keyboard.

Program

```
# Modify records in a file
names = ['Sanjay', 'Sunil', 'Akash', 'Rahul', 'Riddhi', 'Mangal']
f = open('students.txt', 'w+')
for studname in names :
    f.write(studname + '\n')
num = int(input('Enter student number: '))
f.seek(0,0)
i = 1
```

```
while i < num :
    data = f.readline( )
    i += 1

data = f.readline( )
print('Num =', num, 'Name =', data)
f.close( )
```

Output

```
Enter student number: 4
Num = 4 Name = Rahul
```

(i) Assume that a Master file contains two fields, roll number and name of the student. At the end of the year, a group of students join the class and another group leaves. A Transaction file contains the roll numbers and an appropriate code to add or delete a student.

Write a program to create another file that contains the updated list of names and roll numbers. Assume that the Master file and the Transaction file are arranged in ascending order by roll numbers. The updated file should also be in ascending order by roll numbers.

Program

```
# Processing master - transacton files
fm = open('master.txt', 'r')
mdata = fm.readlines( )

ft = open('tran.txt', 'r')
while True :
    trec = ft.readline( )
    if trec == '' :
        break
    tfields = trec.split( )

    if len(tfields) == 2 :
        count = 0
        for record in mdata :
            mfields = record.split( )
            if tfields[0] == mfields[0] :
                break
```

```
            count += 1
        del(mdata[count])

    if len(tfields) == 3 :
        mdata.append(tfields[0] + ' ' + tfields[1] + '\n')

sdata = sorted(mdata)
fp = open('processed.txt', 'w')
for item in sdata :
    print(item)
    item = item.split( )
    rec = item[0] + ' ' + item[1] + '\n'
    fp.write(rec)

fm.close( )
ft.close( )
fp.close( )
```

Output

'master.txt' contains the following records:

A101 Sanjay
A102 Ajay
A103 Anuja
A104 Akhil
A105 Bhushan
A106 Ankit
A107 Vivek
A108 Ankita
A109 Aditi
A110 Harsha

'tran.txt' contains the following records:

A101 D
A105 D
A112 Dheeraj A
A105 Dilip A

'processed.txt' contains the following records after additions and deletions:

A102 Ajay

```
A103 Anuja
A104 Akhil
A105 Dilip
A106 Ankit
A107 Vivek
A108 Ankita
A109 Aditi
A110 Harsha
A112 Dheeraj
```

(j) Given a text file, write a program to create another text file deleting the words "a", "the", "an" and replacing each one of them with a blank space.

Program

```
# Delete file contents selectively
f = open('a.txt', 'r')
data = f.read( )
f.close( )
data = data.replace(' a ', ' ')
data = data.replace(' an ', ' ')
data = data.replace(' the ', ' ')
f = open('b.txt', 'w')
f.write(data)
f.close( )
```

Output

The input file 'a.txt' contains the following text:

```
The world is full of duplicates.
I want an apple a day.
I cannot do the stuff that you want me to do.
```

The output file 'b.txt' contains the following text:

```
The world is full of duplicates.
I want apple day.
I cannot do stuff that you want me to do.
```

24 Logging

Let Us Python Solutions

7th Edition

[A] State whether the following statements are True or False:

(a) It is a good idea to have multiple print statements in a program instead of a log.

Answer

False

(b) Good logs would contain severity level of events that happen during execution of the program.

Answer

True

(c) It is possible to send the logs to console, file or an email.

Answer

True

(d) Only static data of a program can be logged into log files.

Answer

False

(e) Once the log level has been set, only messages above that level would get logged.

Answer

True

(f) It is possible to employ multiple loggers in the same program.

Answer

True

(g) It is possible to employ different loggers in different modules of the same program.

Answer

True

[B] Answer the following questions:

(a) What is the meaning of each parameter in the following call?

```
logging.basicConfig(level = logging.INFO, filename = 'mylog.log',
filemode = 'w', format = '%(asctime)s %(message)s')
```

Answer

All messages including and above INFO severity level would be logged into a file 'mylog.log'. Every time the program is executed the log file will be overwritten. Each log line would contain time stamp and a log message.

(b) What is the meaning of each parameter in the following call?

```
handler = logging.handlers.TimedRotatingFileHandler('mylog.log',
          when = 'M', interval = 4, backupCount = 6)
```

Answer

All messages including and above default severity level would be logged into a file 'mylog.log'. A new log file would be created every 4 seconds and a maximum of 6 log files would be created. Once this count is reached the first log file will be overwritten with the next one that is created and so on. Every time the program is executed

(c) How will you log the values of variables rollno, name, age at INFO level on the console?

Answer

```
logging.info(f'Student date: {rollno} {name} {age}')
```

[C] Attempt the following questions:

(a) Write a program to calculate factorial values of numbers in the range 10 to 15. Log the results into a file.

Program

```
import logging
logging.basicConfig(level = logging.INFO, filename = 'mylog.log',
```

```
                filemode = 'w', format = '%(asctime)s %(message)s')
for num in range(10, 15, 1) :
    fact = 1
    i = 1
    while i <= num :
        fact = fact * i
        i += 1

    logging.info(f'The value of num is {num}')
    logging.info(f'Ant its factorial value is {fact}')
```

Output

```
# Contents of log file mylog.log:
2023-04-21 14:50:18,559 The value of num is 10
2023-04-21 14:50:18,559 Ant its factorial value is 3628800
2023-04-21 14:50:18,559 The value of num is 11
2023-04-21 14:50:18,559 Ant its factorial value is 39916800
2023-04-21 14:50:18,559 The value of num is 12
2023-04-21 14:50:18,559 Ant its factorial value is 479001600
2023-04-21 14:50:18,559 The value of num is 13
2023-04-21 14:50:18,559 Ant its factorial value is 6227020800
2023-04-21 14:50:18,559 The value of num is 14
```

(b) Write a program that infinitely generates 500 random numbers, in the range 100 to 200, one every half a second. Log the numbers generated into rollover log files. A rollover should happen every 4 seconds and a maximum of 5 log files should be created. Terminate the program if the user hits Ctrl-C in the middle of random number generation and log that as a warning.

Program

```
import time
import random
import logging
import logging.handlers

logger = logging.getLogger(__name__)
logger.setLevel(logging.INFO)
handler = logging.handlers.TimedRotatingFileHandler('mylog.log',
            when = 'S', interval = 4, backupCount = 5)
```

```
formatter = logging.Formatter('%(asctime)s %(name)s
                                %(levelname)s %(message)s')
handler.setFormatter(formatter)
logger.addHandler(handler)

try :
    for num in range(500) :
        time.sleep(0.5)
        num = random.randint(100, 200)
        logger.info(f'num = {num}')
except KeyboardInterrupt :
    # handle Ctrl-C
    logging.warning('Cancelled by user')
except Exception as ex :
    # handle unexpected errors
    logging.exception(f'Unhandled error\n{ex}')
finally :
    # stop logging activity
    logging.shutdown( )
```

(c) Write a program that logs messages by sending them to an email account. Hint: Use SMTP handler.

Program

```
import logging
import logging.handlers

logger = logging.getLogger(__name__)
logger.setLevel(logging.DEBUG)

smtph = logging.handlers.SMTPHandler(
    mailhost = ("us2.smtp.mailhostbox.com", 587),
    fromaddr = "kanetkar@kicit.com",
    toaddrs = "kanetkar@kicit.com",
    subject = "Alert!",
    credentials = ('loginname', 'password'),
    secure = None)
smtph.setLevel(logging.ERROR)
formatter = logging.Formatter('%(asctime)s - %(name)s –
                                %(levelname)s - %(message)s')
```

```
smtph.setFormatter(formatter)
logger.addHandler(smtph)

logger.debug('A debug message')
logger.info('An information')
logger.warning('A warning message')
logger.error('An error message')
logger.critical('A message of critical severity')
logging.shutdown( )
```

Output

The emails contain the following log lines:

2023-04-21 12:28:20,006 - __main__ - ERROR - An error message
2023-04-21 12:28:22,758 - __main__ - CRITICAL - A message of critical severity

25 Miscellany

Let Us Python Solutions

7th Edition

[A] State whether the following statements are True or False:

(a) We can send arguments at command-line to any Python program.

Answer

True

(b) The zeroth element of **sys.argv** is always the name of the file being executed.

Answer

True

(c) In Python a function is treated as an object.

Answer

True

(d) A function can be passed to a function and can be returned from a function.

Answer

True

(e) A decorator adds some features to an existing function.

Answer

True

(f) Once a decorator has been created, it can be applied to only one function within the program.

Answer

False

(g) It is mandatory that the function being decorated should not receive any arguments.

Answer

False

(h) It is mandatory that the function being decorated should not return any value.

Answer

False

(i) Type of 'Good!' is bytes.

Answer

False

(j) Type of msg in **msg = 'Good!'** is **str**.

Answer

True

[B] Answer the following questions:

(a) Is it necessary to mention the docstring for a function immediately below the **def** statement?

Answer

Yes

(b) Write a program using command-line arguments to search for a word in a file and replace it with the specified word. The usage of the program is shown below.

C:\> change -o oldword -n newword -f filename

Program

```
# change.py
import sys
import getopt
sys.argv = ['change.py', '-o', 'Unit', '-n', 'UNIT', '-f', 'Syllabus.txt']
if len(sys.argv) != 7 :
    print('Incorrect usage')
    print('change -o oldword -n newword -f filename')
    sys.exit(1)
```

```
try :
    options, arguments = getopt.getopt(sys.argv[1:],'ho:n:f:')
except getopt.GetoptError :
    print('change -o oldword -n newword -f filename')
else :
    for opt, arg in options :
        if opt == '-h' :
            print('change -o oldword -n newword -f filename')
            sys.exit(2)
        elif opt == '-o' :
            oldword = arg
        elif opt == '-n' :
            newword = arg
        elif opt == '-f' :
            filename = arg
    else :
        print('old word:', oldword)
        print('newword: ', newword)
        print('filename:', filename)
        if oldword and newword and filename:
            f = open(filename, 'r')
            data = f.read( )
            f.close( )
            data = data.replace(oldword, newword)
            f = open(filename, 'w')
            f.write(data)
            f.close( )
```

Tips

The program is stored in the file 'change.py'. The file 'syllabus.txt' is present in the same folder as 'change.py'. It contains the following text:

Unit 1 : Object Oriented Programming
Unit 2 : Data encapsulation
Unit 3 : Inheritance
Unit 4 : Polymorphism
Unit 5 : Late binding
Unit 6 : Constructor
Unit 7 : Method overloading

(c) Write a program that can be used at command prompt as a calculating utility. The usage of the program is shown below.

C:\> calc <switch> <n> <m>

Where, **n** and **m** are two integer operands. **switch** can be any arithmetic operator. The output should be the result of the operation.

Program

```
import sys
if len(sys.argv) != 4 :
    print('Incorrect usage')
    print('calc operator number number')
    sys.exit(1)

operator = sys.argv[1]
m = int(sys.argv[2])
n = int(sys.argv[3])
if operator == '+' :
    result = m + n
    print('operator =', operator, 'm =', m, 'n =', n, 'result =', result)
elif operator == '-' :
    result = m - n
    print('operator =', operator, 'm =', m, 'n =', n, 'result =', result)
elif operator == '*' :
    result = m * n
    print('operator =', operator, 'm =', m, 'n =', n, 'result =', result)
elif operator == '/' :
    result = m * n
    print('operator =', operator, 'm =', m, 'n =', n, 'result =', result)
else :
    print('Illegal operator')
```

Output

The program can be executed at command-line as shown below:

C:\>ilde -r calc.py + 23 45

On execution is produces the following output:

operator = + m = 23 n = 45 result = 68

(d) Rewrite the following expressions using bitwise compound assignment operators:

```
a = a | 3        a = a & 0x48        b = b ^ 0x22
c = c << 2       d = d >> 4
```

Answer

```
a |= 3           a &= 0x48           b ^= 0x22
c <<= 2          d >>= 4
```

(e) Consider an unsigned integer in which the rightmost bit is numbered as 0. Write a function **checkbits(x, p, n)** which returns True if all 'n' bits starting from position 'p' are on, False otherwise. For example, **checkbits(x, 4, 3)** will return true if bits 4, 3 and 2 are 1 in number **x**.

Program

```
def display_bits(n) :
    for i in range(7, -1, -1) :
        andmask = 1 << i
        k = n & andmask
        print('0', end = '') if k == 0 else print('1', end = '')
    print( )

def checkbits(x, p, n) :
    no = 0
    for i in range(0, n) :
        if ((x >> (p - 1)) & 1) != 1 :
            return 0
        p -= 1
    return 1

num = int(input('Enter a number between 0 to 255: '))
display_bits(num)
p = int(input('Enter position: '))
n = int(input('Enter number of bits: '))
flag = checkbits(num, p, n)
if flag == 1 :
    print(n, 'bits starting from position', p, 'are on')
else :
    print(n, 'bits starting from position', p, 'are off')
```

Output

```
Enter a number between 0 to 255: 255
11111111
Enter position: 4
Enter number of bits: 3
3 bits starting from position 4 are on
Enter a number between 0 to 255: 96
01100000
Enter position: 6
Enter number of bits: 3
3 bits starting from position 6 are off
```

(f) Write a program to receive a number as input and check whether its 3rd, 6th and 7th bit is on.

Program

```
# Program to check whether 3rd, 6th and 7th bit of a number is on
def display_bits(n) :
    for i in range(7, -1, -1) :
        andmask = 1 << i
        k = n & andmask
        print('0', end = '') if k == 0 else print('1', end = '')

num = int(input('Enter a number between 0 to 255: '))
display_bits(num)
j = num & 0x08
print( )

print('Its third bit is off') if j == 0 else print('Its third bit is on')
j = num & 0x40
print('Its sixth bit is off') if j == 0 else print('Its sixth bit is on')
j = num & 0x80
print('Its seventh bit is off') if j == 0 else print('Its seventh bit is on')
```

Output

```
Enter a number between 0 to 255: 65
01000001
Its third bit is off
Its sixth bit is on
```

Its seventh bit is off

(g) Write a program to receive an 8-bit number into a variable and then exchange its higher 4 bits with lower 4 bits.

Program

```
# Program to exchange a number's higher 4 bits with lower 4 bits
def display_bits(n) :
    for i in range(7, -1, -1) :
        andmask = 1 << i
        k = n & andmask
        print('0', end = '') if k == 0 else print('1', end = '')

num = int(input('Enter a number between 0 to 255: '))
display_bits(num)
n1 = num << 4
n2 = num >> 4
num = n1 | n2
print('\nAfter exchanging bits:')
display_bits(num)
```

Output

```
Enter a number between 0 to 255: 64
01000000
After exchanging bits:
00000100
```

(h) Write a program to receive an 8-bit number into a variable and then set its odd bits to 1.

Program

```
def display_bits(n) :
    for i in range(7, -1, -1) :
        andmask = 1 << i
        k = n & andmask
        print('0', end = '') if k == 0 else print('1', end = '')

def modify_oddbits(n) :
    for i in range(7, -1, -2) :
        ormask = 1 << i
```

```
        n = n | ormask
    return n

num = int(input('Enter a number between 0 to 255: '))
display_bits(num)
num = modify_oddbits(num)
print( )
display_bits(num)
```

Output

```
Enter a number between 0 to 255: 24
00011000
10111010
```

26 Concurrency and Parallelism

Let Us Python Solutions

7th Edition

[A] State whether the following statements are True or False:

(a) Multi-threading improves the speed of execution of the program.

Answer

True

(b) A running task may have several threads running in it.

Answer

True

(c) Multi-processing is the same as multi-threading.

Answer

False

(d) If we create a class that inherits from the **Thread** class, we can still inherit our class from some other class.

Answer

True

(e) It is possible to change the name of the running thread.

Answer

True

(f) To launch a thread, we must explicitly call the function that is supposed to run in a separate thread.

Answer

False

(g) To launch a thread we must explicitly call the **run( )** method defined in a class that extends the **Thread** class.

Answer

False

(h) Though we do not explicitly call the function that is supposed to run in a separate thread, it is possible to pass arguments to the function.

Answer

True

(i) We cannot control the priority of multiple threads that we may launch in a program.

Answer

False

[B] Answer the following questions:

(a) What is the difference between multi-processing and multi-threading?

Answer

Multi-processing is the ability to execute multiple processes simultaneously.

Multi-threading is the ability to execute multiple parts (units) of a program simultaneously.

(b) What is the difference between preemptive multi-threading and cooperative multi-threading?

Answer

Preemptive multi-threading - The OS decides when to switch from one task to another.

Cooperative multi-threading - The task decides when to give up control to the next task.

(c) Which are the two methods available for launching threads in a Python program?

Answer

- By passing a name of the function that should run as a separate thread, to the constructor of the **Thread** class.

- By overriding **__init__( )** and **run( )** methods in a subclass of **Thread** class.

(d) If **Ex** class extends the **Thread** class, then can we launch multiple threads for objects of **Ex** class? If yes, how?

Answer

```
import threading
class Ex(threading.Thread) :
   def __init__(self, s) :
      threading.Thread.__init__(self)
      self.msg = s

   def run(self) :
      while True :
         print(self.msg, end = '\n')

th1 = Ex('Hello')
th1.start( )
th2 = Ex('Hi')
th2.start( )
```

Output

```
HelloHi
HelloHi
HelloHi
HelloHi
HelloHi
HelloHi
HelloHi
... ... ...
```

(e) What do different elements of the following statement signify?

th1 = threading.Thread(target = quads, args = (a, b))

Answer

threading is a module. It contains a **Thread** class.
Object of **Thread** class is being created here.
The address of the object will get stored in **th1**.

quads is the name of the function that will run in a separate thread. **a, b** are the arguments that will be passed to the **quad** function. The arguments must be in the form of a tuple.

(f) Write a multithreaded program that copies contents of one folder into another. The source and target folder paths should be inputted through keyboard.

Program

```
import sys
import threading
import os
import shutil

def copy_file(input_file, output_file):
    shutil.copyfile(input_file, output_file)
    s = input_file + ' copied!\n'
    print(s)

source = sys.argv[1]
target = sys.argv[2]

if not os.path.exists(source) :
    print('source path does not exist')
    exit( )

if not os.path.exists(target) :
    os.mkdir(target)

os.chdir(source)
lst = os.listdir('.')
tharr = [ ]
for file in lst :
    sourcefilepath = source + '\\' + file
    targetfilepath = target + '\\' + file
    th = threading.Thread(target = copy_file, args = (sourcefilepath,
                                        targetfilepath))
    th.start( )
    tharr.append(th)

for th in tharr :
```

```
th.join( )
```

Output

```
c:\Users\Kanetkar\Desktop\sourcedir\cubes.txt copied!
c:\Users\Kanetkar\Desktop\sourcedir\swam.txt copied!
c:\Users\Kanetkar\Desktop\sourcedir\Resolutions.docx copied!
```

(g) Write a program that reads the contents of 3 files a.txt, b.txt and c.txt sequentially and converts their contents into uppercase and writes them into files aa.txt, bb.txt and cc.txt respectively. The program should report the time required in carrying out this conversion. The files a.txt, b.txt and c.txt should be added to the project and filled with some text. The program should receive the file names as command-line arguments. Suspend the program for 0.5 seconds after reading a line from any file.

Program

```
import time
import sys
import threading

start_time = time.time( )
lst1= sys.argv[1:4]
lst2 = sys.argv[4:]

if len(lst1) != 3 or len(lst2) != 3 :
    print('Imporper usage')
    print('Correct usage: convert a.txt b.txt c.txt aa.txt bb.txt cc.txt')
    exit( )

for i in range(0, 3) :
    f1 = open(lst1[i], 'r')
    f2 = open(lst2[i], 'w')
    while True :
        data = f1.readline( )
        if data == '' :
            break
        time.sleep(0.5)
        data = data.upper( )
        f2.write(data)
```

```
    f1.close( )
    f2.close( )
end_time = time.time( )
print('Time required = ', end_time - start_time, 'sec')
```

Output

```
Time required =  4.6332080364227295 sec
```

(h) Write a program that accomplishes the same task mentioned in Exercise [B](g) above by launching the conversion operations in 3 different threads.

Program

```
import time
import sys
import threading

def readFile(input_file, output_file):
    f1 = open(input_file, 'r')
    f2 = open(output_file, 'w')
    while True :
        data = f1.readline( )
        if data == '' :
            break
        data = data.upper( )
        f2.write(data)
        time.sleep(0.5)

start_time = time.time( )
lst1= sys.argv[1:4]
lst2 = sys.argv[4:]

if len(lst1) != 3 or len(lst2) != 3 :
    print('Imporper usage')
    print('Correct usage: convert a.txt b.txt c.txt aa.txt bb.txt cc.txt')
    exit( )

tharr = [ ]
for i in range(0, 3) :
    th = threading.Thread(target = readFile, args = (lst1[i], lst2[i]))
```

```
    th.start( )
    tharr.append(th)

for th in tharr:
    th.join( )

end_time = time.time( )
print('Time required = ', end_time - start_time, 'sec')
```

Output

```
Time required =  1.5756025314331055 sec
```

[C] Match the following:

a. Multiprocessing	1. use multiprocessing module
b. Pre-emptive multi-threading	2. use multi-threading
c. Cooperative multi-threading	3. use threading module
d. CPU-bound programs	4. use multi-processing
e. I/O-bound programs	5. use asyncio module

Answer

Multiprocessing - use multiprocessing module
Pre-emptive multi-threading - use threading module
Cooperative multi-threading - use asyncio module
CPU-bound programs - use multi-processing
I/O-bound programs - use multi-threading

27 Synchronization

Let Us Python Solutions

7th Edition

[A] State whether the following statements are True or False:

(a) All multi-threaded applications should use synchronization.

Answer

False

(b) If 3 threads are going to read from a shared list it is necessary to synchronize their activities.

Answer

False

(c) A **Lock** acquired by one thread can be released by either the same thread or any other thread running in the application.

Answer

True

(d) If **Lock** is used in reentrant code, then the thread is likely to get blocked during the second call.

Answer

True

(e) **Lock** and **RLock** work like a Mutex.

Answer

True

(f) A thread will wait on an **Event** object unless its internal flag is cleared.

Answer

True

(g) A **Condition** object internally uses a lock.

Answer

True

(h) While using **RLock** we must ensure that we call **release( )** as many times as the number of calls to **acquire( )**.

Answer

True

(i) Using **Lock**, we can control the maximum number of threads that can access a resource.

Answer

True

(j) There is no difference between **Event** and **Condition** synchronization objects.

Answer

False

(k) If in a Python program one thread reads a document and another thread writes to the same document, then the two threads should be synchronized.

Answer

True

(l) If in a Python program one thread copies a document and another thread displays progress bar, then the two threads should be synchronized.

Answer

True

(m) If in a Python program one thread lets you type a document, and another thread performs spellcheck on the same document then the two threads should be synchronized.

Answer

True

(n) If in a Python program one thread scans a document for viruses and another thread lets you pause or stop the scan, then the two threads should be synchronized.

Answer

True

[B] Answer the following questions:

(a) Which synchronization mechanisms are used for sharing resources amongst multiple threads?

Answer

Lock, **RLock** and **Semaphore** synchronization mechanisms are used for sharing resources amongst multiple threads.

(b) Which synchronization objects are used for inter-thread communication in a multi-threaded application?

Answer

Event and **Condition** synchronization objects are used for inter-thread communication in a multi-threaded application.

(c) What is the difference between a **Lock** and **RLock**?

Answer

Lock is used to synchronize access to a shared resource.

Rlock is used to synchronize access to a shared resource in reentrant code.

(d) What is the purpose of the **Semaphore** synchronization primitive?

Answer

A semaphore is used to limit access to a resource like network connection or a database server to a limited number of threads.

(e) Write a program that has three threads in it. The first thread should produce random numbers in the range 1 to 20, the second thread should display the square of the number generated by the first thread on the screen, and the third thread should write cube of number generated by first thread into a file.

Program

```
import threading
import random
import queue
import time
import collections

def generate( ) :
    for i in range(10) :
        cond.acquire( )
        num = random.randrange(10, 20)
        print('Generated number =', num)
        qfors.append(num)
        qforc.append(num)
        cond.notifyAll( )
        cond.release( )

def square( ) :
    for i in range(10) :
        cond.acquire( )
        if len(qfors) :
            num = qfors.popleft( )
            print('num =', num, 'Square =', num * num)
        cond.notifyAll( )
        cond.release( )

def cube( ) :
    for i in range(10) :
        cond.acquire( )
        if len(qforc) :
            num = qforc.popleft( )
            f.write('num = ' + str(num) + ' cube = ' +
                        str(num * num * num) + '\n')
        cond.notifyAll( )
```

```
        cond.release( )

f = open('cubes.txt', 'w')
qfors = collections.deque( )
qforc = collections.deque( )
cond = threading.Condition( )
th1 = threading.Thread(target = generate)
th2 = threading.Thread(target = square)
th3 = threading.Thread(target = cube)
th1.start( )
th2.start( )
th3.start( )
th1.join ( )
th2.join( )
th3.join( )
f.close( )
print('All Done!!')
```

Output

```
Generated number = 19
Generated number = 12
Generated number = 16
Generated number = 12
Generated number = 11
Generated number = 10
Generated number = 17
Generated number = 10
Generated number = 19
Generated number = 15
num = 19 Square = 361
num = 12 Square = 144
num = 16 Square = 256
num = 12 Square = 144
num = 11 Square = 121
num = 10 Square = 100
num = 17 Square = 289
num = 10 Square = 100
num = 19 Square = 361
num = 15 Square = 225
All Done!!
```

(f) Suppose one thread is producing numbers from **1** to **n** and another thread is printing the produced numbers. Comment on the output that we are likely to get.

Answer

The output is likely to get mixed up as there is no synchronization between the two threads.

(g) What will happen if thread **t1** waits for thread **t2** to finish and thread **t2** waits for **t1** to finish?

Answer

A deadlock situation would occur.

[C] Match the following pairs:

a. RLock	1. limits no. of threads accessing a resource
b. Event	2. useful in sharing resource in reentrant code
c. Semaphore	3. useful for inter-thread communication
d. Condition	4. signals waiting threads on change in state
e. Lock	5. useful in sharing resource among threads

Answer

RLock - useful in sharing resource in reentrant code
Event - useful for inter-thread communication
Semaphore - limits no. of threads accessing a resource
Condition - signals waiting threads on change in state
Lock - useful in sharing resource among threads

28 Numpy Library

Let Us Python Solutions

7th Edition

[A] State whether the following statements are True or False:

(a) Numpy library gets installed when we install Python.

Answer

False

(b) Numpy arrays work faster than lists.

Answer

True

(c) Numpy array elements can be of different types.

Answer

False

(d) Once created, a Numpy arrays size and shape can be changed dynamically.

Answer

True

(e) **np.array_equal(a, b))** would return **True** if shape and elements of **a** and **b** match.

Answer

True

[B] Answer the following questions:

(a) How will you create a Numpy array of the first 10 natural numbers?

Answer

```
import numpy as np
intarr = np.array([1, 2, 3, 4, 5, 6, 7, 8, 9, 10])
```

(b) Can we create an array of complex numbers using Numpy?

Answer

Yes, as shown below:

```
c = np.array( [[1, 2], [3, 4], [-1, 2]], complex)
```

(c) How would you create 5 arrays each of size 3 x 4 x 5 and fill them with values 0, 1, 5, random and garbage values respectively?

Answer

```
import numpy as np
a1 = np.zeros((3, 4, 5))      # creates 3D array of zeros
a2 = np.ones((3, 4, 5))       # create 3D array of ones
a3 = np.full((3, 4, 5), 5)    # creates 3D array with all values set to 5
a4 = np.empty((3, 4, 5))      # creates 3D array with garbage values
a5 = np.full((3, 4, 5), random.random( ))  # array - random values
```

(d) How would you create a 50-element array and fill it with odd numbers starting from 1?

Answer

```
import numpy as np
a3 = np.linspace(1, 100, 2)
```

(e) How will you obtain the type of elements, number of elements, base address and number of bytes occupied by the following Numpy array?

```
a1 = np.array([1, 2, 3, 4])
```

Answer

```
import numpy as np
a1 = np.array([1, 2, 3, 4])
print(a1.dtype)          # prints int32
print(a1.itemsize)       # prints 4
print(a1.data)           # prints <memory at 0x024BEE08>
print(a1.nbytes)         # prints 16
```

(f) How will you obtain dimensions and shape of the following Numpy array?

```
a1 = np.array([[1, 2, 3, 4], [5, 6, 7, 8])
```

Answer

```
import numpy as np
a1 = np.array([[1, 2, 3, 4],[5, 6, 7, 8]])
print(a1.ndim)
print(a1.shape)
print(a1.size)
```

(g) Given two 3 x 4 matrices how would you add, subtract, multiply and divide corresponding elements of these matrices?

Answer

```
import numpy as np
a1 = np.array([[1, 2, 3, 4],[5, 6, 7, 8], [1, 4, 5, 2]])
a2 = np.array([[1, 1, 1, 1],[2, 2, 2, 2], [3, 3, 3, 3]])
a3 = a1 + a2
a4 = a1 - a2
a5 = a1 * a2
a6 = a1 / a2
```

(h) Which of the following are the scalar arithmetic operations on Numpy array?

```
import numpy as np
a1 = np.array([[10, 2, 3, 4],[5, 6, 7, 8]])
a2 = np.array([[1, 1, 1, 1],[2, 2, 2, 2]])
a3 = a1 + a2
a4 = a1 - a2
a5 = a1 * a2
a6 = a1 / a2
a7 = a1 % a2
a8 = a1 ** 2
a9 += a1
a10 += 5
a11 = a1 + 2
a12 = a1 ** 2
```

Answer

The last three operations are scalar arithmetic operations.

[C] Match the following pairs:

a. s = np.trace(a)	1. Statistical operation
b. s = a.cumsum(axis = 1))	2. Linear algebra operation
c. a2 = np.copy(a1)	3. Deep copy operation
d. print(a1 < 2)	4. Corresponding ele. comparison
e. print(a1 > a2)	5. Comparison with one value
f. print(a[1:3][3:6])	6. Bitwise operation
g. a2 = invert(a1)	7. Slicing operation

Answer

a - 1
b - 2
c - 3
d - 5
e - 4
f - 7
g - 6

29 Matplotlib

Let Us Python Solutions

7th Edition

[A] Answer the following questions:

(a) Write a Python program using Matplotlib to plot linear, quadratic, cubic, and logarithmic growth rates on the same graph. Plot these functions for x ranging from 1 to 10. Ensure all curves are plotted on the same graph. Label the axes, provide a title, and include a legend to differentiate the growth rates.

Program

```
import numpy as np
import matplotlib.pyplot as plt

# define the x values ranging from 1 to 10
x = np.linspace(1, 10, 100)

# define the functions for the different growth rates
y_linear = x                        # linear growth
y_quadratic = x**2                  # quadratic growth
y_cubic = x**3                      # cubic growth
y_logarithmic = np.log(x)           # logarithmic growth

# plot the graphs
plt.figure(figsize=(10, 6))

# plot each growth function
plt.plot(x, y_linear, label="Linear: $f(x) = x$", color='blue')
plt.plot(x, y_quadratic, label="Quadratic: $f(x) = x^2$",
            color='green')
plt.plot(x, y_cubic, label="Cubic: $f(x) = x^3$", color='red')
plt.plot(x, y_logarithmic, label="Logarithmic: $f(x) = log(x)$",
            color='purple')

# label the axes and provide a title
plt.xlabel('x')
plt.ylabel('f(x)')
plt.title('Linear, Quadratic, Cubic, and Logarithmic Growth Rates')

# add a legend
plt.legend( )

# display the graph
plt.grid(True)
plt.show( )
```

Explanation

x values are generated using **np.linspace(1, 10, 100)**, which creates 100 evenly spaced values between 1 and 10. The **plt.plot( )** function is used to plot each function on the same graph. The graph is titled, and the x/y axes are labeled, with a legend to identify each curve. **plt.grid(True)** adds a grid to the plot to make it more readable.

Output

The output will be a plot with four curves as shown below.

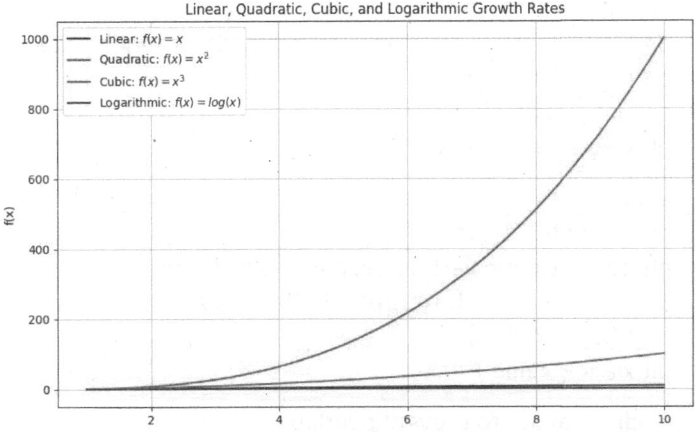

(b) Write a Python program using Matplotlib to generate a Dot Plot, Histogram and Box Plot. You need to generate a random dataset of 100 values following a normal distribution with a mean of 50 and a standard deviation of 10. Create a single figure with three subplots:

A Dot Plot for the dataset.
A Histogram with 10 bins.
A Box Plot for the dataset.

Label the axes and provide appropriate titles for each plot.

Program

```
import numpy as np
import matplotlib.pyplot as plt

# generate random data following a normal distribution
```

```
data = np.random.normal(loc=50, scale=10, size=100)

# create a figure with 3 subplots: dot plot, histogram, and box plot
plt.figure(figsize=(12, 8))

# dot plot (scatter plot)
plt.subplot(3, 1, 1)
plt.plot(np.arange(len(data)), data, 'bo')  # 'bo' makes the dots blue
                                            # x-values are indices
plt.title('Dot Plot')
plt.xlabel('Index of Data Points')
plt.ylabel('Value')

# histogram
plt.subplot(3, 1, 2)
plt.hist(data, bins=10, color='orange', edgecolor='black')
plt.title('Histogram')
plt.xlabel('Value')
plt.ylabel('Frequency')

# box Plot
plt.subplot(3, 1, 3)
plt.boxplot(data, vert=False, patch_artist=True,
                  boxprops=dict(facecolor='lightblue'))
plt.title('Box Plot')
plt.xlabel('Value')

# adjust layout to prevent overlap
plt.tight_layout( )

# display the graph
plt.show( )
```

Explanation:

A dataset of 100 values is generated using the statement **np.random.normal(loc=50, scale=10, size=100)**. This creates random data with a mean of 50 and a standard deviation of 10, resembling a normal distribution.

The first subplot shows a Dot Plot using **plt.plot( )**.

We have used **np.arange(len(data))** for the x-values, which represents the index of each data point. This way, the points are spread vertically, and each data point is represented clearly.

The second subplot displays a Histogram using **plt.hist( )**, where the data is divided into 10 bins, and the frequencies of each bin are plotted.

The third subplot creates a Box Plot using **plt.boxplot( )**, which shows the median, quartiles, and potential outliers in the dataset. The box plot is displayed horizontally by setting vert=False.

plt.subplot(3, 1, ..) divides the figure into three vertical sections, one for each plot. **plt.tight_layout( )** ensures that the subplots don't overlap and have proper spacing.

Output

The Dot Plot will show data points on a scatter plot where the x-axis is the index of each data point, and the y-axis is the value of the data.

The Histogram will display the frequency distribution of the dataset in 10 bins.

The Box Plot will visualize the distribution, quartiles, and outliers of the dataset.

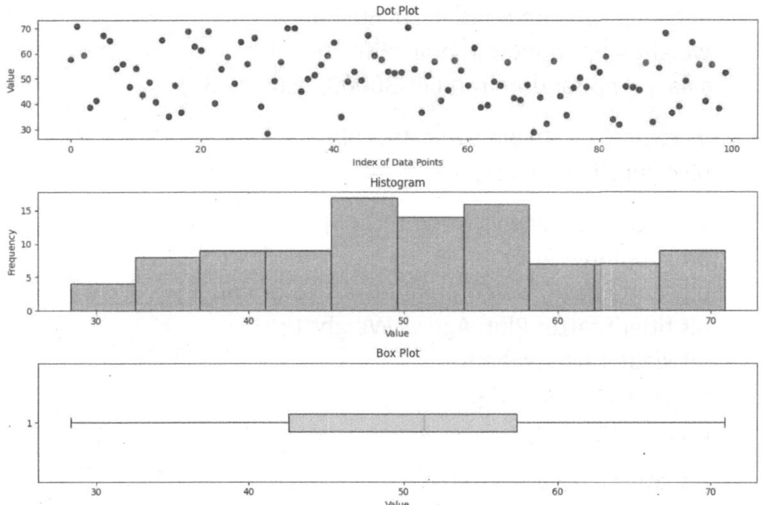

(c) Suppose we have data about the age, weight (in kgs), and salary of a group of individuals working in a company. We are interested in finding out the relationships between these variables. We wish to find out whether there is any relationship between age and weight. If yes, we want to know whether it is positive or negative, strong or weak, linear or non-linear. Similarly, we want to explore whether there is any relationship between age and salary.

Create two scatter plots:

The first plot should show the relationship between age and weight using dots (.) as markers.

The second plot should show the relationship between age and salary using stars (*) as markers.

Each data point represents an individual, and the scatter plot will help visualize the possible relationships between the variables.

Program

```
import numpy as np
import matplotlib.pyplot as plt

# generating random data for the example
np.random.seed(0)  # for reproducibility

# random data for 50 individuals
age = np.random.randint(20, 60, 50)
weight = np.random.randint(50, 100, 50)
salary = np.random.randint(30000, 120000, 50)

# create a figure with 2 scatter plots
plt.figure(figsize=(12, 6))

# scatter plot: age vs weight
plt.subplot(1, 2, 1)
plt.scatter(age, weight, marker='.', color='blue')
plt.title('Scatter Plot: Age vs Weight')
plt.xlabel('Age (years)')
plt.ylabel('Weight (kg)')
plt.grid(True)

# scatter plot: age vs salary
plt.subplot(1, 2, 2)
plt.scatter(age, salary, marker='*', color='green')
plt.title('Scatter Plot: Age vs Salary')
plt.xlabel('Age (years)')
```

```
plt.ylabel('Salary ($)')
plt.grid(True)

# adjust layout and display the plots
plt.tight_layout( )
plt.show( )
```

Explanation

We have simulated random data for 50 individuals with three variables: age (20–60 years), weight (50–100 kg), and salary (30k–120k).

The first scatter plot shows the relationship between age and weight using dots (.). The second scatter plot shows the relationship between age and salary using stars (*).

Each scatter plot has appropriate titles and labels for the axes. **plt.tight_layout( )** ensures the two plots do not overlap and have proper spacing.

Output

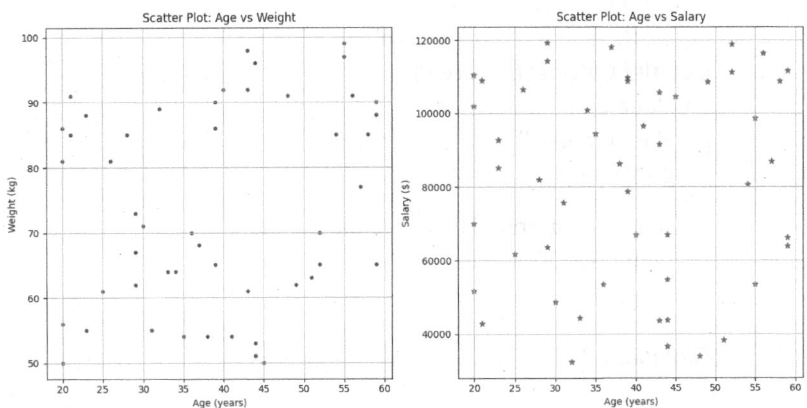

(d) Write a Python program using Matplotlib to plot a tangent and a cotangent curve in two different subplots. Each curve should be drawn using 100 x-coordinates between 0.1 and 2π (slightly above 6.28). The tangent curve should be plotted in the first subplot and the cotangent curve in the second subplot.

Program

```
import numpy as np
import matplotlib.pyplot as plt

# generate 100 x-coordinates between 0.1 and 2π
x = np.linspace(0.1, 2 * np.pi, 100)

# compute the tangent and cotangent values for each x-coordinate
y_tan = np.tan(x)     # tangent of x
y_cot = 1 / np.tan(x)  # cotangent of x

# create a figure with 2 subplots
plt.figure(figsize=(12, 6))

# plot tangent curve
plt.subplot(1, 2, 1)
plt.plot(x, y_tan, color='blue')
plt.title('Tangent Curve')
plt.xlabel('x')
plt.ylabel('tan(x)')
plt.grid(True)

# plot cotangent curve
plt.subplot(1, 2, 2)
plt.plot(x, y_cot, color='green')
plt.title('Cotangent Curve')
plt.xlabel('x')
plt.ylabel('cot(x)')
plt.grid(True)

# adjust layout and display the plots
plt.tight_layout( )
plt.show( )
```

Explanation

We have generated 100 evenly spaced x-coordinates between 0.1 and 2π (about 6.28) using **np.linspace(0.1, 2 * np.pi, 100)**. This range avoids singularities at 0 and π for the cotangent curve.

The tangent values are computed using **np.tan(x)** and cotangent values using **1/np.tan(x)** for the same x-coordinates.

The first **subplot (plt.subplot(1, 2, 1))** plots the tangent curve. The second **subplot (plt.subplot(1, 2, 2))** plots the cotangent curve.

plt.tight_layout( ) ensures the subplots are properly spaced. Grids are added using **plt.grid(True)** for better visualization.

Output

The tangent and cotangent curves will help us visualize the behavior of the tangent and cotangent functions over the specified range.

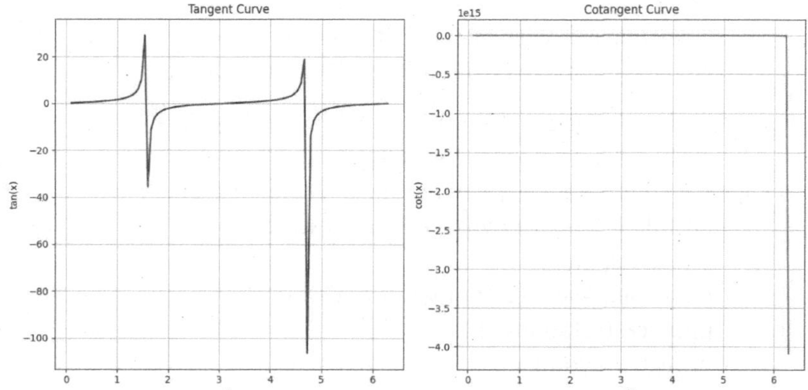

(e) Suppose we have data about cities, their average temperature, population density, and annual rainfall. The data is stored in a CSV file called city_data.csv. The file has the following structure:

City,Temperature,Population Density,Rainfall
New York,13.3,10933,1200
Los Angeles,18.5,3276,380
Chicago,10.2,4600,990
Houston,20.8,3613,1260
Phoenix,22.3,3120,210
Denver,9.5,1750,400
Miami,25.1,4771,1570
Boston,11.4,5260,1140
Seattle,10.8,3534,1520
San Francisco,14.0,2754,670

Write a program to plot a bar graph showing city-wise average temperatures. Also, create a grouped bar graph to show the population density of each city and the annual rainfall of each city.

Program

```
import pandas as pd
import matplotlib.pyplot as plt
import numpy as np

# load the data from 'data.csv'
data = pd.read_csv('data.csv')

# plotting city-wise average temperature
city_temperatures = data[['City', 'Temperature']]

plt.figure(figsize=(10, 6))
plt.bar(city_temperatures['City'],
city_temperatures['Temperature'], color='skyblue')
plt.title('City-wise Average Temperature')
plt.xlabel('City')
plt.ylabel('Average Temperature (°C)')
plt.xticks(rotation=45)
plt.tight_layout( )
plt.show( )

# plot population density and rainfall for each city
population_rainfall = data[['City', 'Population Density', 'Rainfall']]

# create a grouped bar chart
fig, ax1 = plt.subplots(figsize=(10, 6))

bar_width = 0.35
index = np.arange(len(population_rainfall['City']))

# population density bar
bar1 = ax1.bar(index, population_rainfall['Population Density'],
bar_width, label='Population Density', color='lightcoral')

# create a second axis for rainfall
ax2 = ax1.twinx()
bar2 = ax2.bar(index + bar_width, population_rainfall['Rainfall'],
bar_width, label='Rainfall (mm)', color='lightgreen')

# set labels and titles
ax1.set_xlabel('City')
```

```
ax1.set_ylabel('Population Density (people per sq km)')
ax2.set_ylabel('Annual Rainfall (mm)')
plt.title('City-wise Population Density and Rainfall')
ax1.set_xticks(index + bar_width / 2)
ax1.set_xticklabels(population_rainfall['City'], rotation=45)

# add legend
ax1.legend(loc='upper left')
ax2.legend(loc='upper right')

plt.tight_layout( )
plt.show( )
```

Explanation

The program uses pandas to load the data from 'data.csv' file into a DataFrame. Each row contains a city's name, its average temperature, population density, and annual rainfall.

We have extracted the cities and their respective temperatures from the data, and used **plt.bar( )** to create a bar graph showing the average temperature for each city. The cities are displayed on the x-axis, and the temperatures are on the y-axis.

The program groups the population density and rainfall of each city using a grouped bar chart. Two y-axes are used—one for population density and the other for rainfall. The **twinx( )** method is used to plot the two bars side by side for each city, with one bar representing population density and the other representing rainfall.

plt.tight_layout( ) ensures the subplots have proper spacing and don't overlap. Legends are added for clarity.

Output

The output provides clear visualizations of temperature distribution and how cities compare in terms of population density and rainfall.

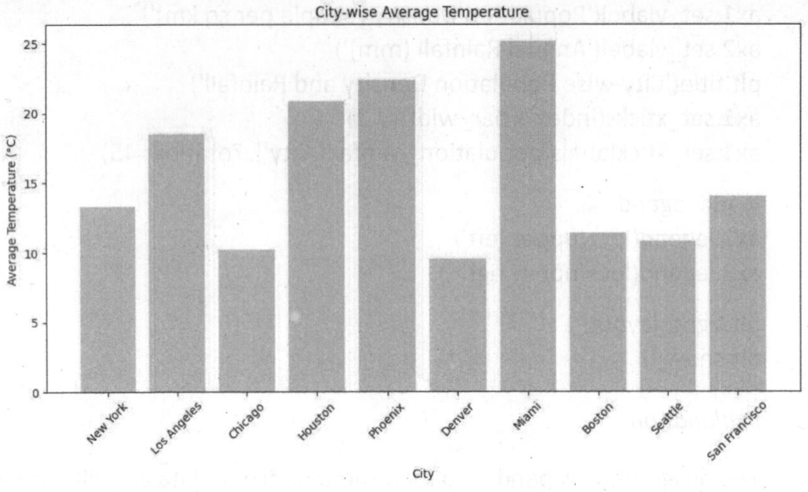
City-wise Average Temperature
Average Temperature (°C)
0
5
10
15
20
25
New York
Los Angeles
Chicago
Houston
Phoenix
Denver
Miami
Boston
Seattle
San Francisco
City

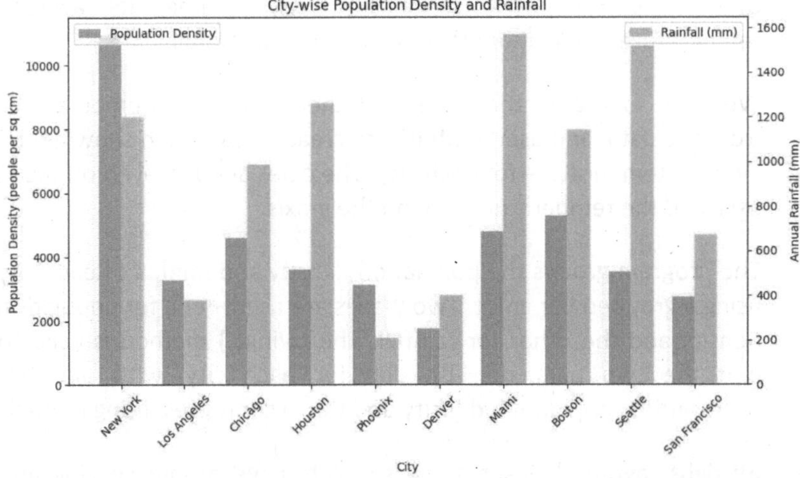
City-wise Population Density and Rainfall
Population Density
Rainfall (mm)
Population Density (people per sq km)
0
2000
4000
6000
8000
10000
Annual Rainfall (mm)
0
200
400
600
800
1000
1200
1400
1600
New York
Los Angeles
Chicago
Houston
Phoenix
Denver
Miami
Boston
Seattle
San Francisco
City

30 Pandas Library

Let Us Python Solutions

7th Edition

[A] State which Pandas function will you use to perform the following operations:

(a) Read data from a .csv file.

Answer

read_csv( )

(b) Combine data from two DataFrames.

Answer

merge( ), concat( )

(c) Count the number of rows that meet a particular criterion.

Answer

sum( ) with a condition
Example: (df['column'] > value).sum( )

(d) Organize the data in a DataFrame into different categories based on a particular criterion.

Answer

groupby( )

(e) Pick only the first row from a set of rows.

Answer

head(1)

(f) Access a range of values from a Series.

Answer

loc[ ]

(g) Access a range of values from using positions of values.

Answer

iloc[ ]

[B] Answer the following questions:

(a) Data of all deliveries bowled across all IPL seasons is available in the file 'deliveries.csv'. Write a program to obtain the following information:
- Total runs scored
- Total wickets fallen
- Batting strike rate
- Bowling strike rate

Program

```
import pandas as pd
df = pd.read_csv('deliveries.csv')
tot_runs = sum(df['total_runs'])
tot_wkts = sum(df['is_wicket'])
print('Total runs scored =', tot_runs)
print('Total wickets fallen =', tot_wkts)

total_runs = sum(df['total_runs'])
total_deliveries = len(df)
batting_strike_rate = total_runs / total_deliveries * 100
print('Batting strike rate:', batting_strike_rate)

wkt_deliveries = sum(df['is_wicket'])
bowling_strike_rate = total_deliveries / wkt_deliveries
print('Bowling strike rate:', bowling_strike_rate)
```

Output

```
Total runs scored = 347756
Total wickets fallen = 12950
Batting strike rate: 133.28069906484745
Bowling strike rate: 20.148262548262547
```

(b) Data of all deliveries bowled across all IPL seasons is available in the file 'deliveries.csv', and data of all matches in all IPL seasons is present in 'matches.csv'. Write a program to obtain the following information:
- Total runs scored per IPL season
- Batting strike rate per season

Program

```
import pandas as pd
df1 = pd.read_csv('matches.csv')
df2 = pd.read_csv('deliveries.csv')

# total runs per season
mergeddf = df2.merge(df1, left_on = 'match_id', right_on = 'id')
total_runs_per_season = mergeddf[['season', 'total_runs']]
    .groupby(by = ['season']).sum( )
print('Total runs per season:')
print(total_runs_per_season.reset_index( )
    .to_string(index=False, header=False))

# batting strike rate per season
runs_per_season = mergeddf[['season', 'total_runs']]
    .groupby(by = ['season']).sum( )
deliveries_per_season = mergeddf[['season', 'total_runs']]
    .groupby(by = ['season']).count( )
batting_strike_rate_per_season = runs_per_season /
    deliveries_per_season * 100
print('Batting strike rate per season:')
print(batting_strike_rate_per_season.reset_index( )
    .to_string(index=False, header=False))
```

Output

```
Total runs per season:
2007/08   17937
   2009   16353
2009/10   18883
   2011   21154
   2012   22453
   2013   22602
   2014   18931
   2015   18353
   2016   18862
   2017   18786
   2018   19901
   2019   19434
2020/21   19416
   2021   18637
   2022   24395
```

```
   2023   25688
   2024   25971
```

```
Batting strike rate per season:
2007/08   132.975017
   2009   120.189622
2009/10   130.245551
   2011   124.340210
   2012   126.374740
   2013   124.343951
   2014   132.384615
   2015   134.434515
   2016   133.811010
   2017   135.521570
   2018   139.304214
   2019   135.788150
2020/21   133.360808
   2021   129.199307
   2022   136.193613
   2023   143.805632
   2024   151.850553
```

Explanation

Calculating Total Runs per Season:

The 'deliveries.csv' (ball-by-ball data) is merged with the 'matches.csv' (match data) using the **match_id** from 'deliveries.csv' and **id** from 'matches.csv' using the **merge( )** function. This step enriches the ball-by-ball data with match-specific details such as the season.

mergeddf[['season', 'total_runs']].groupby(by = ['season']).sum( ) groups the merged data by season and sums the **total_runs** for each season. This gives the total runs scored in each IPL season.

reset_index( ) is used to convert the groupby object back into a DataFrame and remove the grouping index.

The result is printed without displaying index numbers or headers using **to_string(index=False, header=False)**.

Calculating Batting Strike Rate per Season:

Runs per season: This is the same as in the previous section. **runs_per_season** stores the total runs for each season.

mergeddf[['season', 'total_runs']].groupby(by = ['season']).count( ) counts the number of deliveries (balls faced) for each season, by counting the occurrences of **total_runs** in each season. This essentially gives the total number of balls bowled in each season.

The strike rate is calculated as **(runs_per_season / deliveries_per_season) * 100**, which gives the batting strike rate for each season. The strike rate measures the number of runs scored per 100 balls.

(c) Data of all deliveries bowled across all IPL seasons is available in the file 'deliveries.csv' and data of all matches in all IPL seasons is present in 'matches.csv'. Write a program to obtain the following information:

- Find Orange Cap holder of each season (batter who scores maximum runs in a season)
- Find Purple Cap holder of each season (bowler who takes maximum wickets in a season)

Program

```
import pandas as pd
df1 = pd.read_csv('matches.csv')
df2 = pd.read_csv('deliveries.csv')

mergeddf = df2.merge(df1, left_on = 'match_id', right_on = 'id')

# Orange Cap Holder
maxruns_scorer_per_season = mergeddf
    .groupby(['season', 'batter'])['batsman_runs'].sum( )
    .sort_values(ascending = False)
    .reset_index( )
    .drop_duplicates(subset = 'season', keep = 'first')
    .sort_values('season')
print(maxruns_scorer_per_season.to_string(index=False))

# Purple Cap Holder
maxwkts_per_season = mergeddf
    .groupby(['season', 'bowler'])['is_wicket'].sum( )
    .sort_values(ascending = False)
```

```
    .reset_index( )
    .drop_duplicates(subset = 'season', keep = 'first')
    .sort_values('season')
print(maxwkts_per_season. to_string(index=False))
```

Output

season	batter	batsman_runs
2007/08	SE Marsh	616
2009	ML Hayden	572
2009/10	SR Tendulkar	618
2011	CH Gayle	608
2012	CH Gayle	733
2013	MEK Hussey	733
2014	RV Uthappa	660
2015	DA Warner	562
2016	V Kohli	973
2017	DA Warner	641
2018	KS Williamson	735
2019	DA Warner	692
2020/21	KL Rahul	676
2021	RD Gaikwad	635
2022	JC Buttler	863
2023	Shubman Gill	890
2024	V Kohli	741

season	bowler	is_wicket
2007/08	Sohail Tanvir	24
2009	RP Singh	26
2009/10	PP Ojha	22
2011	SL Malinga	30
2012	M Morkel	30
2013	DJ Bravo	34
2014	MM Sharma	26
2015	DJ Bravo	28
2016	B Kumar	24
2017	B Kumar	28
2018	AJ Tye	28
2019	K Rabada	29
2020/21	K Rabada	32
2021	HV Patel	35
2022	YS Chahal	29

```
2023          MM Sharma          31
2024          HV Patel           30
```

Explanation

Orange Cap Holder (Max Runs Scorer in Each Season):

df2.merge(df1, left_on='match_id', right_on='id') merges the two DataFrames on the columns match_id (from deliveries.csv) and id (from matches.csv), which essentially adds the season and other match details to the deliveries dataset. The resulting DataFrame mergeddf contains both ball-by-ball data as well as match-specific details like season, venue, etc.

mergeddf.groupby(['season', 'batter'])['batsman_runs'].sum( ) groups the data by season and batter and sums the batsman_runs for each combination. This gives the total runs scored by each batter in each season.

.sort_values(ascending=False) sorts the summed runs in descending order, so the batter with the most runs in each season is at the top.

.reset_index( ) flattens the grouped data into a new DataFrame with columns **season**, **batter**, and **batsman_runs**.

.drop_duplicates(subset='season', keep='first') keeps only the first occurrence of each season after sorting, which gives the batter with the maximum runs for each season (the Orange Cap holder).

.sort_values('season') sorts the DataFrame by season so the output shows each season in chronological order.

print(maxruns_scorer_per_season.to_string(index=False)) prints the resulting DataFrame, showing the Orange Cap holder for each season without any row numbers (index).

Purple Cap Holder (Max Wicket Taker in Each Season):

mergeddf.groupby(['season', 'bowler'])['is_wicket'].sum( ) groups the data by season and bowler and sums the **is_wicket** column, which has values of 1 for each wicket taken. This gives the total wickets taken by each bowler in each season.

.sort_values(ascending=False) sorts the summed wickets in descending order, so the bowler with the most wickets in each season is at the top.

.reset_index( ) flattens the grouped data into a new DataFrame with columns season, bowler, and **is_wicket** (total wickets).

.drop_duplicates(subset='season', keep='first') keeps only the first occurrence of each season after sorting, which gives the bowler with the maximum wickets for each season (the Purple Cap holder).

.sort_values('season') sorts the DataFrame by season so the output shows each season in chronological order.

print(maxwkts_per_season.to_string(index=False)) prints the resulting DataFrame, showing the Purple Cap holder for each season without any row numbers (index).

(d) Data of all deliveries bowled across all IPL seasons is available in the file 'deliveries.csv' and data of all matches in all IPL seasons is present in 'matches.csv'. Write a program to obtain the following information:
- Top 5 batters who have scored maximum runs across all seasons
- Top 3 bowlers who have taken maximum wickets across all seasons

Program

```
import pandas as pd

# load the data
df1 = pd.read_csv('matches.csv')
df2 = pd.read_csv('deliveries.csv')

# merge the datasets on match_id and id to combine match and
# delivery-level data
mergeddf = df2.merge(df1, left_on='match_id', right_on='id')

# top 5 batters who have scored the max runs across all seasons
top_batters = mergeddf.groupby('batter')['batsman_runs']
    .sum( ).sort_values(ascending=False).head(5).reset_index( )
print("Top 5 Batters with Maximum Runs:")
print(top_batters.to_string(index=False))

# top 3 bowlers who have taken the max wickets across all seasons
# filter out only dismissals that count as wickets
```

```
# exclude run-outs, and others
# is_wicket = 1 indicates a wicket
wickets = mergeddf[mergeddf['is_wicket'] == 1]
top_bowlers = wickets.groupby('bowler')['is_wicket']
    .sum( ).sort_values(ascending=False).head(3).reset_index( )
print("\nTop 3 Bowlers with Maximum Wickets:")
print(top_bowlers.to_string(index=False))
```

Output

```
Top 5 Batters with Maximum Runs:
        batter        batsman_runs
       V Kohli                8014
      S Dhawan                6769
     RG Sharma                6630
     DA Warner                6567
      S K Raina               5536

Top 3 Bowlers with Maximum Wickets:

        bowler           is_wicket
     YS Chahal                 213
      DJ Bravo                 207
     PP Chawla                 201
```

Explanation

Batters' Runs: We use **groupby('batter')** to group the data by batter and then use **sum( )** to calculate the total runs scored by each batter. The top 5 batters are selected by sorting in descending order using **sort_values(ascending=False)** and selecting the top 5 using **head(5)**.

Bowlers' Wickets: We filter the dataset to include only deliveries where is_wicket == 1, which indicates that a wicket was taken (excluding run-outs and other non-bowler dismissals). Then, we use **groupby('bowler')** and **sum( )** to calculate the total number of wickets taken by each bowler. The top 3 bowlers are selected in the same way by sorting and using **head(3)**.

(e) Using data from 'matches.csv' and 'deliveries.csv' define a function that receives the name of a batter and returns the name of the team against which the batter has scored maximum number of runs.

Program

```
import pandas as pd

# function to find team against which a batter has scored most runs
def team_against_max_runs(batter_name) :
    # load the CSV files
    matches_df = pd.read_csv('matches.csv')
    deliveries_df = pd.read_csv('deliveries.csv')

    # merge the deliveries and matches data on match_id (left join)
    merged_df = deliveries_df.merge(matches_df,
        left_on='match_id', right_on='id')

    # filter the data for the given batter
    batter_data = merged_df[merged_df['batter'] == batter_name]

    # group the data by the opponent team and sum the runs
    runs_against_teams = batter_data
        .groupby('bowling_team')['batsman_runs'].sum( )

    # find the team against which the batter scored the most runs
    max_runs_team = runs_against_teams.idxmax( )

    return max_runs_team

# Example usage
batter_name = 'V Kohli'
result = team_against_max_runs(batter_name)
print(f"The team against which {batter_name} has scored the most
runs is: {result}")
```

Output

The team against which V Kohli has scored the most runs is: Chennai Super Kings

(f) Using data from 'matches.csv' and 'deliveries.csv' define a function that receives the name of a bowler and returns the name of the team against which the bowler has taken maximum number of wickets.

Program

```
import pandas as pd

# Function to find team against which bowler has taken most wkts
def team_against_max_wickets(bowler_name) :
    # load the CSV files
    matches_df = pd.read_csv('matches.csv')
    deliveries_df = pd.read_csv('deliveries.csv')

    # merge the deliveries and matches data on match_id (left join)
    merged_df = deliveries_df
        .merge(matches_df, left_on='match_id', right_on='id')

    # filter the data for the given bowler
    bowler_data = merged_df[merged_df['bowler'] ==
        bowler_name]

    # check if the bowler has any deliveries in the dataset
    if bowler_data.empty :
        return f"No data found for bowler: {bowler_name}"

    # filter for rows where a wicket was taken (is_wicket = 1)
    wickets_data = bowler_data[bowler_data['is_wicket'] == 1]

    # check if the bowler has taken any wickets
    if wickets_data.empty :
        return f"{bowler_name} has not taken any wickets."

    # group by opponent team and count the number of wickets
    wickets_against_teams = wickets_data
        .groupby('batting_team')['is_wicket'].sum( )

    # check if the groupby result is empty
    # to avoid calling idxmax on an empty series
    if wickets_against_teams.empty:
    return f"{bowler_name} has no recorded wickets against any
        team."

    # find the team against which the bowler took the most wickets
    max_wickets_team = wickets_against_teams.idxmax( )

    return max_wickets_team

# Example usage
bowler_name = 'DJ Bravo'  # replace with any bowler's name
result = team_against_max_wickets(bowler_name)
```

```
print(f"The team against which {bowler_name} has taken the most wickets is: {result}")
```

Output

The team against which DJ Bravo has taken the most wickets is: Mumbai Indians

(g) Using data from 'matches.csv' and 'deliveries.csv' define a function that receives the name of a batter and returns the name of the team against which the batter has hit maximum number of fours and sixes.

Program

```
import pandas as pd

def team_against_max_boundaries(batter_name) :
    # load the CSV files
    matches_df = pd.read_csv('matches.csv')
    deliveries_df = pd.read_csv('deliveries.csv')

    # merge deliveries and matches data on 'match_id'
    merged_df = deliveries_df
        .merge(matches_df, left_on='match_id', right_on='id')

    # filter the data for the given batter
    batter_data = merged_df[merged_df['batter'] == batter_name]

    # check if the batter exists in the dataset
    if batter_data.empty :
        return f"No data found for batter: {batter_name}"

    # Filter for fours and sixes
    fours_data = batter_data[batter_data['batsman_runs'] == 4]
    sixes_data = batter_data[batter_data['batsman_runs'] == 6]

    # group by bowling_team and count the number of 4s and 6s
    fours_against_teams = fours_data
        .groupby('bowling_team')['batsman_runs'].count( )
    sixes_against_teams = sixes_data
        .groupby('bowling_team')['batsman_runs'].count( )

    # combine fours and sixes for each team
    total_boundaries_against_teams = fours_against_teams
        .add(sixes_against_teams, fill_value=0)
```

```
    # check if there are any boundaries
    if total_boundaries_against_teams.empty :
        return f"{batter_name} has not hit any fours or sixes."

    # find the team against which the batter has hit most boundaries
    max_boundaries_team = total_boundaries_against_teams
        .idxmax( )

    return max_boundaries_team

# Example usage
batter_name = 'V Kohli'  # replace with any batter's name
result = team_against_max_boundaries(batter_name)
print(f"The team against which {batter_name} has hit the most
fours and sixes is: {result}")
```

Output

The team against which V Kohli has hit the most fours and sixes is: Chennai Super Kings

(h) Write a program to create a DataFrame containing names of animals and their approximate weights. Export the data in this DataFrame to a file 'sample.csv'. The file should contain headers 'Name' and 'Weight' in its first row.

Program

```
import pandas as pd
lst = [['Dog', 20], ['Cat', 14], ['Cow', 125]]
df = pd.DataFrame(lst, columns=['Name', 'Weight'])
df.to_csv('sample.csv')
```

31 Security Programming

Let Us Python Solutions

7th Edition

[A] Match the pairs:

(a) Integrity	(1) Signing, Verification
(b) Authenticity	(2) Encryption / Decryption
(c) Confidentiality	(3) SHA256
(d) Non-repudiation	(4) MD5

Answer

(a)– (3), (b) – (4), (c) – (2), (d) - (1)

[B] Pick the correct choice:

(a) Which of the following techniques will you use if you wish to transmit a file ensuring its confidentiality.

(1) Use asymmetric encryption for encryption/decryption
(2) Use symmetric encryption for encryption/decryption
(3) Use asymmetric encryption for sharing symmetric key, use symmetric encryption/decryption for file
(4) Use symmetric encryption for sharing symmetric key, use asymmetric encryption/decryption for file

Answer

(3) Use asymmetric encryption for sharing symmetric key, use symmetric encryption/decryption for file

(b) We wish to download a file from the server and check whether it has been downloaded correctly or not. Which technique would you employ to achieve this?

(1) Download the file, compute its SHA256 checksum
(2) Download the file, compute its SHA256 checksum, compare this checksum with checksum of file reported on server
(3) Download the file using RSA
(4) Use symmetric encryption while downloading the file

Answer

(2) Download the file, compute its SHA256 checksum, compare this checksum with checksum of file reported on server

[C] Answer the following questions:

(a) Which are the four aspects of security? Does every secure application need to implement them?

Answer

Four aspects of security are Integrity, Authenticity, Confidentiality and Non-repudiation. Every secure application may need one or more of them.

(b) Obtain MD5 checksum of the following strings and check whether they are same:

"Six slippery snails slid slowly seaward."
"Six silppery snails slid slowly seaward."

Program

```
from cryptography.hazmat.primitives import hashes
from cryptography.hazmat.backends import default_backend

def get_sha256_openssl(input_string):
   # create a SHA256 hash object
   digest = hashes.Hash(hashes.SHA256( ),
               backend=default_backend( ))

   # update the hash object with the bytes of the input string
   digest.update(input_string.encode('utf-8'))

   # finalize the hash and get the result
   return digest.finalize( ).hex( )

str1 = "Six slippery snails slid slowly seaward." ;
str2 = "Six silppery snails slid slowly seaward." ;
chksum1 = get_sha256_openssl(str1)
chksum2 = get_sha256_openssl(str2)
print( "String1:", str1 )
print( "Checksum1:", chksum1)
print( "String2:", str1 )
print( "Checksum2:", chksum2)
```

(c) Obtain SHA256 checksum of any executable file.

Program

```
from cryptography.hazmat.primitives import hashes
from cryptography.hazmat.backends import default_backend
```

```
# function to calculate the SHA-256 hash of a file
def sha256_of_file(file_path):
    # create a SHA-256 hash object
    digest = hashes.Hash(hashes.SHA256( ),
                         backend=default_backend( ))

    # open file in binary mode and read it in chunks
    f = open(file_path, "rb")
    chunk_size = 4096
    while 1 :
        chunk = f.read(chunk_size)
        if not chunk :
            break
        digest.update(chunk)

    f.close( )
    # finalize the hash and return the digest
    return digest.finalize( ).hex( )

file_path = "humor.exe"
chksum = sha256_of_file(file_path)
print("SHA-256 Hash:", chksum)
```

32 Interaction With ChatGPT

Let Us Python Solutions

7th Edition

[A] Answer the following questions:

(a) Arrange the following steps involved in making a HTTP request in correct sequence:

(1) Set the response variable
(2) Set the POST method
(3) Set the URL for POST request
(4) Set the POST data
(5) Set the necessary custom headers

Answer

The correct sequence of steps involved in making a HTTPS request is as follows:
(1) Set the URL for POST request
(2) Set the necessary custom headers
(3) Set the POST data
(4) Set the POST method
(5) Set the response variable

(b) How does ChatGPT API authenticate a user request made through a HTTP call?

Answer

ChatGPT API authenticates a user request made through an HTTP call by requiring an API key. This key, provided by OpenAI, must be included in the request's headers as a bearer token. Specifically, the header should be formatted as Authorization: Bearer YOUR_API_KEY. The server uses this key to verify the identity of the user and determine if he/she has the necessary permissions to access the API, ensuring secure and authenticated interactions.

(c) Which are the ways to interact with ChatGPT?

Answer

There are two main ways to use ChatGPT—interactively and programmatically:

Interactively: Visit the OpenAI website at https://chatgpt.com to engage with ChatGPT in real-time by typing prompts and receiving responses. This user-friendly method requires no technical setup and is perfect for casual use.

Programmatically: Advanced users can access ChatGPT via its API, integrating its capabilities into their applications. This approach allows for automation, customization, and embedding ChatGPT into chatbots, virtual assistants, or any app requiring natural language processing.

[B] Attempt the following questions:

(a) Write a program to convert a given text into an audio file. Use the following information to make the HTTP request.

Endpoint - https://api.openai.com/v1/audio/speech

model - string containing Text to Speech model name tts-1 or tts-1-hd

input - string containing the text to generate audio for (maximum length is 4096 characters)

voice - string containing the voice to use when generating the audio. Supported voices are alloy, echo, fable, onyx, nova, and shimmer

Program

```
import requests
import os

api_key = "INSERT YOUR API KEY HERE"
tts_endpoint = "https://api.openai.com/v1/audio/speech"

# Function to convert text to audio using OpenAI API
def text_to_audio(model, text, voice, fname="audio.mp3") :
    # set  the headers
    hdrs = {
            "Authorization": f"Bearer {api_key}",
            "Content-Type": "application/json"
        }

    # data to be sent to the API
    data = { "model": model, "input": text, "voice": voice }

    try :
```

```
        # make the POST request to the API
        response = requests.post(tts_endpoint,
                            headers=hdrs, json=data)

        # check if the request was successful
        if response.status_code == 200 :
            # save the audio content to a file
            with open(fname, "wb") as audio_file :
                audio_file.write(response.content)
            print(f"Audio saved to {fname}")
        else :
            print( "Failed to generate audio")
    except Exception as e :
        print( f"An error occurred: {str(e)}")

# example usage
if __name__ == "__main__" :
    model = "tts-1"
    text = "Hello, this is a simple sample text for conversion."
    voice = "alloy"  # Or 'alloy', 'echo', 'fable', 'onyx', 'nova'
    text_to_audio(model, text, voice)
```

(b) Write a program to generate 4 images of birds flying in the sky with a computer's mouse in their beak. Use the following information to make the HTTP request.

Endpoint - https://api.openai.com/v1/images/generations

prompt - string describing the image to be drawn by the model

input - string containing the text to generate audio for (maximum length is 4096 characters)

n - Number of images to be drawn

size - Size of the image

Program

```
import requests
import json

api_url = https://api.openai.com/v1/images/generations
api_key = "INSERT YOUR API KEY HERE"

# define the prompt and other parameters
```

```
prompt = "Draw a picture showing birds flying in the sky with a
computer's mouse in their beak"

# set up the headers with the API key
hdrs = {
        "Authorization": f"Bearer {api_key}",
        "Content-Type": "application/json"
    }

# set up the data to send in the POST request
data = {
        "prompt": prompt,
        "n": 4,  # number of images to generate
        "size": "256x256"  # size of the image
    }

# send the POST request to the API
response = requests.post(api_url, headers=hdrs,
                    data=json.dumps(data))

# check if the request was successful
if response.status_code == 200 :
    response_data = response.json( )
    # loop through all the generated image URLs
    print("Generated Image URLs:")
    for i, image_data in enumerate(response_data['data']):
            image_url = image_data['url']
            print(f"Image {i+1}: {image_url}")
else :
    print("Failed to generate image")
    print(response.text)
```

Output

4 URLs will be generated and printed. If you paste each URL in browser, you will get the following images:

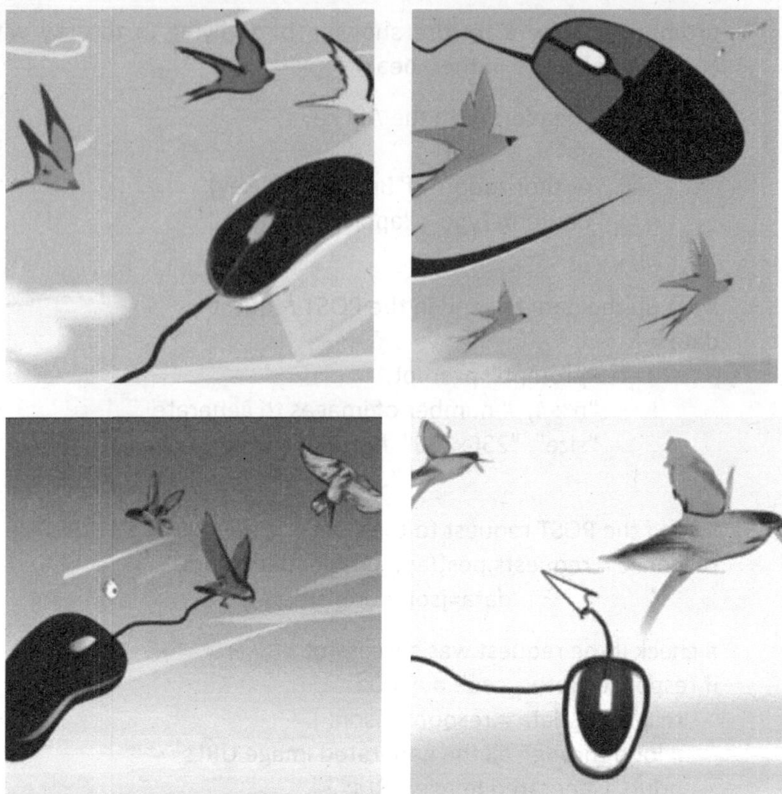

(c) Write a program to analyze a given sentence with a view to detect the mood of the sentence. For example, the mode of the sentence "I am so impressed by your performance" is "admiration and appreciation". Use the following information to make the HTTP request.

Endpoint - https://api.openai.com/v1/chat/completions

model - string containing the model name gpt-3.5-turbo

messages - A list of messages comprising the conversation

Program

```
import requests
import json

api_key = "INSERT YOUR API KEY HERE"
```

```
api_url = "https://api.openai.com/v1/chat/completions"

# define the message to analyze the mood of the sentence
message = "What is the mood of this text: I am so impressed by
your performance"

# create the payload for the API request
payload = {
                "model": "gpt-3.5-turbo",
                "messages": [
                        {
                            "role": "user",
                            "content": message
                        }
                    ],
                "max_tokens": 50
        }

# set up headers with authorization
hdrs = {
        "Authorization": f"Bearer {api_key}",
        "Content-Type": "application/json"
    }

# send POST request to the API
response = requests.post(api_url, headers=hdrs,
                data=json.dumps(payload))

# check if the request was successful
if response.status_code == 200  :
    response_data = response.json( )
    mood = response_data['choices'][0]['message']['content']
    print(f"Detected Mood: {mood}")
else :
    print( "Request failed")
    print(response.text)
```

Output

Detected Mood: The mood of this text is positive and admiring.

Periodic Tests

Let Us Python Solutions

7th Edition

Periodic Test I
(Based on Chapters 1 to 6)

Time: 90 Minutes Maximum Marks: 40

[A] Fill in the blanks: [5 Marks, 1 Mark each]

(1) In Python every entity is treated as object.

(2) Python has 33 keywords.

(3) The function used to obtain address of an object is id( ).

(4) The function used to find out whether a variable is of int type is type( ).

(5) The three varieties of types in Python are Basic, Container and User-defined.

[B] State True or False: [5 Marks, 1 Mark each]

(1) In Python there is no need to define type of a variable.

True

(2) In Python an int can have any arbitrary value.

True

(3) A single line comment in Python language starts with # sign.

True

(4) Effect of switch statement can be obtained using if - elif -else.

True

(5) There is no do-while loop in Python.

True

[C] What would be the output of the following programs:
[5 Marks, 1 Mark each]

(1) print(6 // 2)

Output

3

(2) print(3 % -2)

Output

-1

(3) print(-2 % -4)

Output

-2

(4) print(17 / 4)

Output

4.25

(5) print(-5 // -3)

Output

1

[D] Point out the error, if any, in the following programs: [5 Marks, 1 Mark each]

(1)
```
import math
x = 2
print(math.sqrt(x))
```

No error

(2)
```
msg = 'C:\\newfolder\\newfile'
print('msg')
```

No error.

(3)
```
a = 4
b = 2
if a = b :
```

```
   print('Equal')
else :
   print('Unequal')
```

Error. Use == instead of =.

(4)
```
lst = ['00', '01', '02', '03']
i = 0
while i < len(lst) :
    print(i, lst[i])
    i += 1
```

No error

(5)
```
lst = ['Lion', 'Tiger', 'Wolf', 'Cheetah']
for i, ele in enum(lst) :
    print(i, ele)
```

Error. Use enumerate( ) function, there is no function enum( ).

[E] Attempt the following questions: [20 Marks, 5 Marks each]

(1) Write a program to enter the numbers till the user wants and at the end it should display the count of positive, negative and zeros entered.

Program

```
# Count number of positives, negatives and zeros
ans = 'y'
pos = neg = zero = 0
while ans == 'y' or ans == 'Y' :
   num = int(input('Enter a number: '))
   if num == 0 :
      zero += 1
   elif num > 0 :
      pos += 1
   elif num < 0 :
      neg += 1
   ans = input('Do you want to continue? ')
print('You entered', pos, 'positive numbers')
```

```
print('You entered', neg, 'negative numbers')
print('You entered', zero, 'zeros')
```

(2) Write a program to find the range of a set of numbers that are input through the keyboard. Range is the difference between the smallest and biggest number in the list.

Program

```
# Program to find the range of a set of numbers
import sys
tot = int(input("Enter total no. of numbers "))
i = 0
small = sys.maxsize
big = -sys.maxsize
while i < tot :
    n = int(input("Enter a number: "))
    if n < small :
        small = n
    if n > big :
        big = n
    i += 1

range = big - small
print('Range = ', range)
```

(3) If three integers are entered through the keyboard, write a program to determine whether they form a Pythagorean triplet or not.

Program

```
a = int(input('Enter a number: '))
b = int(input('Enter a number: '))
c = int(input('Enter a number: '))
if a * a == b * b + c * c or b * b == a * a + c * c or
    c * c == a * a + b * b :
      print('Numbers form a Pythagorean triplet')
else :
      print('Numbers do not form a Pythagorean triplet')
```

(4) Write a program to calculate sum of first 10 terms of the following series:

1! 2! + 2! 3! + 3! 4! + 4! 5! + ... + 9! 10!

Program

```
for i in range(1, 11) :
    prod1 = 1
    s = 0
    for j in range(1, i + 1) :
        prod1 = prod1 * j

    prod2 = prod1 * (j + 1)
    term = prod1 * prod2
    print(prod1, prod2)
    s = s + term
print ( 'sum of series = ', s )
```

Periodic Test II
(Based on Chapters 7 to 11)

Time: 90 Minutes Maximum Marks: 40

[A] Answer the following questions: [5 Marks, 1 Mark each]

(1) How will you create an empty list, empty tuple, empty set and empty dictionary?

Answer

```
lst = [ ]
tpl = ( )
s = set( )
dct = { }
```

(2) What is the difference between a set and a frozenset?

Answer

A set's elements can change, a frozenset's elements cannot change.

(3) What is wrong with the set s = {[10, 20, 30], (10, 20, 30)}?

Answer

A set cannot contain a list as one of its element.

(4) How will you convert the list [10, 20, 30, 40, 10, 30] into a list [40, 10, 20, 30] without using del( ) or remove( ) method?

Answer

```
lst = list(set(lst))
```

(5) How will you print a float centrally justified in 10 columns, with 3 places beyond decimal point?

Answer

```
print(f'{round(a,3):^{10}}')
```

[B] State True or False: [5 Marks, 1 Mark each]

(1) Similar elements are usually stored in a set.

False

(2) Dissimilar elements are usually stored in a list.

False

(3) Key - value pairs are usually stored in a tuple.

False

(4) Unique elements are usually stored in a dictionary.

False

(5) Raw strings are used to format the output in a print( ) function.

False

[C] Match the following: [5 Marks, 1 Mark each]

(a) Dictionary	(1) a = set( )
(b) Tuple	(2) x = { }
(c) Set	(3) b = 'msg'
(d) List	(4) d = (10, 20, 30)
(e) String	(5) f = [10, 20, 30]

Answer

(a) - (2)
(b) - (4)
(c) - (1)
(d) - (5)
(e) - (3)

[D] Point out the error, if any, in the following programs:
[5 Marks, 1 Mark each]

(1)
```
l, b, h = input('Enter length, breadth & height: ')
print(l, b, h)
```

Answer

Error: too many values to unpack

(2)
```
lst = [11, 10, 5, 77, 24]
lst.add(45)
print(lst)
```

Answer

Error: 'list' object has no attribute 'add'

(3)
```
tpl = ((1, 5), (2, 3), (4, 5))
for x, y in tpl :
   print(x, y)
```

Answer

No error

(4)
```
s = {77, 41, 22}
s.del(41)
print(s)
```

Answer

Error: del( ) cannot be called using s

(5)
```
dct = { 'Lion' : 4, 'Tiger' : 2, 'Wolf' : 9, 'Cheetah' : 1 }
for k, v in dct.keys( ) :
    print(k, v)
```

Answer

Error: too many values to unpack

[E] Attempt the following questions: [20 Marks, 5 Marks each]

(1) Write a program to receive the value of radius of a circle and calculate and print its area and circumference. Make sure that both values are printed in 15 columns each with 2 places beyond decimal point.

Program

```
r = int(input('Enter radius of circle: '))
a = round(3.14 * r * r, 2)
c = round(2 * 3.14 * r, 2)
print(f'Area = {a:15} {Circumference = }{c:15}')
```

Output

```
Enter radius of circle: 5
Area =          78.5 Circumference =          31.4
```

(2) A dictionary contains roll number as key and first name, middle name and last name as values. Write a program to print the dictionary items in alphabetical order by first name.

Program

```
import operator
d1 = {
        'A101' : ('Rahul', 'Ajay', 'Joshi'),
        'A102' : ('Ramesh', 'Atul', 'John'),
        'A121' : ('Ritesh', 'Abhin', 'Kate'),
        'A111' : ('Rajesh', 'Akash', 'Zade')
    }
d2 = dict(sorted(d1.items( ), key = operator.itemgetter(1)))
print(d2)
```

Output

```
{'A101': ('Rahul', 'Ajay', 'Joshi'), 'A111': ('Rajesh', 'Akash', 'Zade'),
'A102': ('Ramesh', 'Atul', 'John'), 'A121': ('Ritesh', 'Abhin', 'Kate')}
```

(3) A tuple contains tuples of book title and author. Write a program to print the titles and author names with first letter of each word in capital and rest in small case.

Program

```
tpl = ( ('Principles of programming', 'rahul ajay joshi'),
        ('Art of computer science', 'donald e knuth'),
        ('Modern algebra', 'Ritesh abhin KATE') )
for t in tpl :
```

```
print(t[0].title( ), t[1].title( ))
```

Output

```
Principles Of Programming Rahul Ajay Joshi
Art Of Computer Science Donald E Knuth
Modern Algebra Ritesh Abhin Kate
```

(4) A list contains numbers. One of these numbers occurs only once, all others occur twice. Write a program to identify the number which occurs only once.

Program

```
lst = [10, 20, 30, 10, 40, 30, 20, 50, 60, 50, 60]
s = set(lst)
for num in s :
    c = lst.count(num)
    if c == 1 :
        print(num, 'occurs only once')
        break
```

Output

```
40 occurs only once
```

Periodic Test III
(Based on Chapters 12 to 17)

Time: 90 Minutes Maximum Marks: 40

[A] State True or False: [5 Marks, 1 Mark each]

(1) We cannot create a tuple using comprehension.

True

(2) A Python function can receive Positional arguments, Keyword arguments, Variable-length positional arguments and Variable-length keyword arguments.

True

(3) When we execute a program its module name is __module__ and it is available in the variable __name__.

True

(4) Functions show( ) and display( ) defined in a module functions can be used by importing them using the statement:

import show, display

False

(5) For a directory to be treated as a package it must contain a file named __init__.py in it.

True

[B] Answer the following questions: [10 Marks, 1 Mark each]

(1) How will you receive 4 numbers as input from keyboard using list comprehension?

Answer

```
n1, n2, n3, n4 = [int(n) for n in input('Enter four values: ').split( )]
```

(2) How will you generate 20 random numbers in the range 10 to 100 using list comprehension?

Answer

```
import random
a = [random.randrange(10, 100) for n in range(20)]
```

(3) How will you generate the following list using comprehension?

[[25, 125], [36, 216], [49, 343], [64, 512], [81, 729], [100, 1000]]

Answer

```
a = [[n, n * n] for n in range(5, 11)]
```

(4) How will you create a set even numbers in the range 10 to 30 using comprehension?

Answer

```
a = [n for n in range(10, 30) if n % 2 == 0]
```

(5) How will you delete all numbers having a value between 20 and 50 from the following list using comprehension?

lst = [10, 3, 4, 5, 15, 20, 21, 23, 46, 50]

Answer

```
lst1 = [n for n in lst if n < 20 or n > 50]
```

(6) Using dictionary comprehension how will you convert

d = {'AMOL': 20, 'ANIL': 12, 'SUNIL': 13, 'RAMESH': 10}

into

{'Amol': 400, 'Anil': 144, 'Sunil': 169, 'Ramesh': 100}

Answer

```
d = {k.capitalize( ) : v ** 2 for (k, v) in d.items( )}
```

(7) Consider the following code snippet:

```
def print_it(a, b, c, d, e) :
    print(a, b, c, d, e)

tpl = ('A', 'B', 'C', 'D', 'E')
```

How will you pass all elements of a tuple **t** to a function **print_it( )**?

Answer

```
print_it(*tpl)
```

(8) Consider the following code snippet:

```
def print_it(i, j, *args, x, y, **kwargs) :
    pass

print_it(10, 20, 100, 200, x = 30, y = 40)
```

What gets passed to **args** and **kwargs**?

Answer

100, 200 go to args, nothing goes to kwargs

(9) If a function **cal_sum( )** receives **3 integers** and returns their **sum**, which of the following calls to a function **cal_sum( )** are acceptable?

i. sum = cal_sum(a, b, c)
ii. print(cal_sum(a, b, c))
iii. sum = cal_sum(a, calSum(25, 10, 4), b)

Answer

i, ii, iii and iv

(10) Consider the following code snippet:

```
def print_it(**kwargs) :
    pass

dct = {'Student' : 'Ajay', 'Age' : 23}
```

Which is the CORRECT way to pass dct to **print_it( )**?

Answer

```
print_it(**dct)
```

[C] Attempt the following questions: [20 Marks, 5 Marks each]

(1) Write a program that converts list of temperature in Celsius degrees to equivalent Fahrenheit using list comprehension.

Program

```
celsius = [32, 40, 25, 45, 18]
farh = [(e * 9 /5) + 32 for e in celsius]
print(farh)
```

Output

```
[89.6, 104.0, 77.0, 113.0, 64.4]
```

(2) Write a recursive function to obtain sum of first 25 natural numbers.

Program

```
def resum(num) :
    if num == 1 :
        return num
    return num + resum(num - 1)

print('Sum of first 25 numbers: ', resum(25))
```

Output

```
Sum of first 25 numbers:  325
```

(3) A string is entered through the keyboard. Write a recursive function that counts the number of capital letters in this string.

Program

```
def count_caps(s, count) :
    if s == '' :
        return count

    if s[0] >= 'A' and s[0] <= 'Z' :
        count += 1

    count = count_caps(s[1:], count)
    return count

c = count_caps('Cidade de Goa', 0)
print('Count of caps = ', c)
```

Output

```
Count of caps = 2
```

(4) Write a program using functional programming to prepend a string 'Hi ' to every element in a list of strings.

Program

```
lst1 = ['Shrinivas', 'Savitri', 'Shanmukh', 'Shweta']
lst2 = map(lambda s : 'Hi ' + s, lst1)
for item in lst2 :
    print(item)
```

Output

```
Hi Shrinivas
Hi Savitri
Hi Shanmukh
Hi Shweta
```

(5) Suppose a dictionary contains names of students and marks obtained by them in an examination. Write a program using

functional programming to obtain a list of students who obtained less than 40 marks in the examination.

Program

```
dct = {'Shrinivas' : 35, 'Savitri' : 45, 'Shanmukh' : 38, 'Shweta' : 42}
lst2 = filter(lambda x : x[1] < 40, dct.items( ))
for item in lst2 :
   print(item)
```

Output

```
('Shrinivas', 35)
('Shanmukh', 38)
```

Periodic Test IV
(Based on Chapters 18 to 21)

Time: 90 Minutes | Maximum Marks: 40

[A] Fill in the blanks: [4 Marks, 1 Mark each]

(1) Every class is derived from an object class.

(2) Inheritance and Containership reuse mechanisms are provided in Python.

(3) When we are using containership, we are doing byte code level reuse.

(4) Generator functions create iterators.

[B] State True or False: [12 Marks, 1 Mark each]

(1) Construction of an object always proceeds from derived towards base.

False

(2) From an abstract class an object cannot be created.

True

(3) On calling an instance method of an object, address of the object always gets passed to it.

True

(4) Iterable(s) cannot be passed to a zip( ) function.

False

(5) In containership an object is nested inside another object.

True

(6) +, - and * operators have been overloaded in str class.

False

(7) The + operator has been overloaded in str, list and int classes.

True

(8) It is possible to call a global function, another class method and instance method from a class method?

True

(9) The size of the object is influenced by instance data, class data, global data and local variables.

False

(10) Class methods can access class data and global data.

True

(11) If NewSample class is derived from Sample class and an object of NewSample is created then __init__( ) of Sample class followed by __init__( ) of NewSample class will be called.

True

(12) A generator expression generates the next element on demand, rather than generating all elements upfront.

True

[C] Attempt the following questions: [14 Marks, 1 Mark each]

(1) Separate the following into classes and objects:

Bird, Player, Crow, Raj, Eagle, Flower, Rose, Lily, Flute, Instrument

Answer

Class - Bird, Player, Flower, Instrument
Object - Crow, Raj, Eagle, Rose, Lily, Flute

(2) How will you create an object of a Trial class?

Answer

```
t = Trial( )
```

(3) Which of the following can be done with regards to a class?

i. A class can be inherited from another class
ii. A class can be defined inside another class

Answer

Both, i and ii

(4) What does the following code do?

```
e = Sample( )
```

Answer

Allocates space for the object of type Sample and calls the constructor function

(5) What happens when control returns from fun( )?

```
def func( ) :
    s = new Trial( )
```

Answer

__del__( ) method gets called.

(6) How many arguments will be passed to the __init__( ) in the following statement?

```
t = Trial(10, 3.14, 'Hello')
```

Answer

4

(7) How many times does the __init__( ) of Student class get called on execution of the following code snippet?

```
lst = [ ]
lst.append(Sample('Raju', 25))
lst.append(Sample('Anand', 34))
```

Answer

2 times

(8) How should show( ) be defined in Example class?

```
e = Example( )
e.show('A', '3.14, 10, 20, 30)
```

Answer

```
def class Example :
    def show(self, a, b, c, d) :
            pass
```

(9) To overload the % operator, which method should be defined in the corresponding class?

Answer

__mod__( )

(10) To overload the //= operator, which method should be defined in the corresponding class?

Answer

__ifloordiv__( )

(11) How will you prevent a new class to get inherited from an existing class Employee?

Answer

There is no mechanism in Python to do this

(12) Suppose a base class contains two instance variables x, y and one class variable **z**. A class derived from it contains an instance variable **a** and two class variables **b** and **c**. What will the derived class object contain?

Answer

x, y, a

(13) What does an __iter__( ) function of list or str return?

Answer

An iterator object

(14) What will be the output of the following code snippet?

```
lst = ['A', 20, 'C', 4.50]
item = lst.__iter__( )
print(item.__next__( ))
```

Answer

A

[D] Attempt the following questions: [10 Marks, 5 Marks each]

(1) Write a program that implements a Person class containing name, and age. Derive a class Student from Person class and maintain roll number and marks in 3 subjects in it. Create a list of 5 Student objects and fill them with suitable values through the class constructors. Define a class method display( ) to print the list contents on the screen.

Program

```
class Person :
    def __init__(self, n, a) :
        self._name = n
        self._age = a

    def display(self) :
        print(self._name, self._age, end = ' ')

class Student(Person) :
    def __init__(self, n, a, r, m1, m2, m3) :
        super( ).__init__(n, a)
        self._rollno = r
        self._marks1 = m1
        self._marks2 = m2
        self._marks3 = m3
```

```
    def display(self) :
        super( ).display( )
        print(self._rollno, self._marks1, self._marks2, self._marks3)

lst = [ ]
s = Student('Smita', 23, 'A101', 45, 50, 55)
lst.append(s)
s = Student('Shiela', 24, 'A111', 55, 60, 55)
lst.append(s)
s = Student('Shailesh', 23, 'S123', 45, 56, 75)
lst.append(s)
s = Student('Shekhar', 25, 'A144', 56, 65, 65)
lst.append(s)
s = Student('Shyam', 23, 'S177', 75, 50, 59)
lst.append(s)
for item in lst :
    item.display( )
```

Output

```
Smita 23 A101 45 50 55
Shiela 24 A111 55 60 55
Shailesh 23 S123 45 56 75
Shekhar 25 A144 56 65 65
Shyam 23 S177 75 50 59
```

(2) Create two lists, one containing names of fruits and another containing their corresponding weights. Write a program to take the two lists as input and create a dictionary containing name of fruit as the key and weight as value.

Program

```
lst1 = ['Guava', 'Mango', 'Grape', 'Banana']
lst2 = [150, 200, 15, 180]
d = {k : v for (k, v) in zip(lst1, lst2)}
print(d)
```

Output

```
{'Guava': 150, 'Mango': 200, 'Grape': 15, 'Banana': 180}
```

Periodic Test V
(Based on Chapters 22 to 26)

Time: 90 Minutes | Maximum Marks: 40

[A] Fill in the blanks: [5 Marks, 1 Mark each]

(1) A Python decorator begins with @ symbol.

(2) Arguments passed to a Python script are available in variable sys.argv.

(3) The command-line arguments passed to a script can be parsed using getopt( ) function.

(4) In Unicode every character is assigned an integer value called code point which are usually expressed in hexadecimal.

(5) Communicate between threads can be done using Event or Condition object.

[B] State True or False: [10 Marks, 1 Mark each]

(1) In Parallelism multiple threads are running at the same time.

True

(2) In Concurrency, at any given time only one thread is running.

True

(3) Performance of I/O-bound program can improve if different units of the program are executed in overlapping times.

True

(4) Performance of a CPU-bound program can improve with parallelism.

True

(5) A 100-meter race is a good example of Concurrency.

False

(6) Order of except blocks matters.

True

(7) Assertion performs run-time checks of assumptions.

True

(8) Serialization means writing objects to a file.

True

(9) 'r+' and 'w+' modes are same as both permit reading from and writing to a file.

False

(10) When 'with' keyword is used for opening a file, the file gets closed as soon as its usage is over.

True

[C] Answer the following questions: [10 Marks, 1 Mark each]

(1) Which out of syntax error, logical error and exception occurs at the time of execution?

Answer

exception

(2) How will you apply a decorator @yk_decorator to a function fun( )?

Answer

```
@yk_decorator
def fun( ) :
    pass
```

(3) Consider the following code snippet:

```
def yk_decorator(func) :
    def wrapper( ) :
```

```
print('###############')
func( )
print('###############')
```

which statement will you add at the end of this code snippet to make the decorator work?

Answer

return wrapper

(4) If we execute a script as

C:\>sample.py cat dog parrot

how will you access 'C:\>sample.py'?

Answer

sys.argv[0]

(5) If a script is executed as

C:\>filecopy.py -s sourcefilename -t targetfilename

then how will you parse the arguments using getopt( ) function?

Answer

options = getopt.getopt(sys.argv[1:],'s:t:')

(6) What will be the output of the following code snippet?

```
import sys, getopt
sys.argv =['C:\\a.py', '-h', 'word1', 'word2']
options, arguments = getopt.getopt(sys.argv[1:],'s:t:h')
print(options)
print(arguments)
```

Answer

```
[('-h', '')]
['word1', 'word2']
```

(7) How will you launch a function fun( ) in a thread and pass arguments a, b, c to it?

Answer

```
th1 = threading.Thread(target = squares, args = (a, b))
```

(8) How will you check whether 5th and 7th bit in num are on or off?

Answer

```
if num & 32 == 1 and num & 128 == 1 :
    print('bits 5 and 7 are on')
```

(9) How will you store a hexadecimal value E0A485 in a bytes data type?

Answer

```
by = b'\xe0\xa4\x85'
```

(10) How many except blocks will you write if same action is to be taken in case of 3 exceptions?

Answer

Only one except clause should be written with the 3 exceptions mentioned in a tuple

[D] Attempt the following questions: [20 Marks, 5 Marks each]

(1) Write a program that defines a function to calculate the value of c using following formula:

c = ((a + b) / (a - b))

Program

```
def compute(a, b) :
   try :
      c = ((a + b) / (a - b))
   except ZeroDivisionError :
      print('Denominator is 0!!')
   else :
      print('c =', c)

a = int(input('Enter any integer: '))
```

```
b = int(input('Enter any integer: '))
c = compute(a, b)
```

Output

```
Enter any integer: 12
Enter any integer: 10
c = 11.0
```

(2) A file 'sent.txt' contains multiple lines, each containing multiple words. Write a program to find the longest words in the file.

Program

```
def longest_word(fname) :
    f = open(fname, 'r')
    words = f.read( ).split( )
    print(words)
    big = len(max(words, key = len))
    return [w for w in words if len(w) == big]

print(longest_word('sent.txt'))
```

Output

```
['Bad', 'officials', 'are', 'elected', 'by', 'good', 'citizens', 'who', 'do',
'not', 'vote', 'Good', 'citizens', 'is', 'a', 'rare', 'breed', 'Having', 'one',
'child', 'makes', 'you', 'a', 'parent', 'Having', 'two', 'you', 'are', 'a',
'referee', 'There', 'is', 'always', 'life', 'beyond', 'work', 'and',
'entertainment', 'Your', 'communication', 'skills', 'are', 'vital',
'Divisibility', 'of', 'integer', '9']

['entertainment', 'communication']
```

(3) Define a decorator function @timer which calculates the time required to execute any function. Use this decorator to time the function factorial( ) while calculating factorial values of 7, 10 and 25.

Program

```
import time
def timer(func) :
```

```
    def calculate(*args, **kwargs) :
        start_time = time.perf_counter( )
        value = func(*args, **kwargs)
        end_time = time.perf_counter( )
        runtime = end_time - start_time
        print(f'Finished {func.__name__!r} in {runtime:.8f} secs')
        return value
    return calculate

@timer
def factorial(num) :
   p = i = 1
   while i <= num :
      p = p * i
      i += 1
   return(p)

f = factorial(7)
print('Factorial of 7 = ', f)
f = factorial(10)
print('Factorial of 10 = ', f)
f = factorial(25)
print('Factorial of 25 = ', f)
```

Output

```
Finished 'factorial' in 0.00000599 secs
Factorial of 7 =  5040
Finished 'factorial' in 0.00000813 secs
Factorial of 10 =  3628800
Finished 'factorial' in 0.00001583 secs
Factorial of 25 =  15511210043330985984000000
```

OTHER TITLES OF INTEREST

Learn Autonomous Programming with **Python**
ISBN: 9789355517630

Learn Python Game Development with **ChatGPT**
ISBN: 9789355516435

Basics of **Python Programming**
ISBN: 9789355516404

Python Programming for **Students**
ISBN: 9789355516084

Modern Data Mining with **Python**
ISBN: 9789355519146

Implementing Statistics with **Python**
ISBN: 9789355517104

Ultimate Data Science Programming in **Python**
ISBN: 9789365895667

Learn Python Generative AI
ISBN: 9789355518972

Python
Quick Interview Guide
ISBN: 9789389423303

Mastering Search Algorithms with **Python**
ISBN: 9789355516244

Modern Python Programming using **ChatGPT**
ISBN: 9789365894318

Python for **Finance**
ISBN: 9789355516893

Test Your Skills in Python - 2nd Edition
ISBN: 9789355511812

MCQ for **Python Users**
ISBN: 9789355517739

Python for **Cybersecurity** Cookbook
ISBN: 9789355513809

Advanced Python Guide
ISBN: 9789355516756